SPECULATION AND MONOPOLY IN URBAN DEVELOPMENT: ANALYTICAL FOUNDATIONS WITH EVIDENCE FOR TORONTO

J. R. Markusen and D. T. Scheffman

Speculation and Monopoly in Urban Development: analytical foundations with evidence for Toronto

PUBLISHED FOR THE ONTARIO ECONOMIC COUNCIL BY
UNIVERSITY OF TORONTO PRESS
TORONTO AND BUFFALO

Canadian Cataloguing in Publication Data

Markusen, James R., 1948-
   Speculation and monopoly in urban development

   (Ontario Economic Council research studies; 10)

   Bibliography: p.
   ISBN 0-8020-3348-2

   1. Land subdivision. 2. Land subdivision – Ontario –
   Toronto metropolitan area. 3. Real estate investment.
   4. Cities and towns – Planning. I. Scheffman, David T.,
   1943- II. Title. III. Series: Ontario Economic
   Council. Ontario Economic Council research studies;
   10.
   HD257.M36   333.7'7   C77-001386-4

$5 7, /24$

This study reflects the views of the authors and not necessarily those of
the Ontario Economic Council.

This book has been published during the
Sesquicentennial year of the University of Toronto

Contents

vi Contents

Acknowledgments

This study was funded by the Ontario Economic Council whose support is gratefully acknowledged. A great many individuals contributed to our effort including municipal planners, developers, realtors, and government officials who gave freely of their time. Participants in two review seminars at the Ontario Economic Council and members of the urban economics workshop at the University of Western Ontario were especially helpful in their comments and suggestions on our preliminary efforts. John Bossons of the University of Toronto in particular deserves to be singled out for his careful reading of and comments on successive drafts. Gordon Davies, Mark Frankena, John Palmer, and Arthur Robson of the University of Western Ontario deserve our thanks as does George Fallis of the Ontario Economic Council for helping us carry out this project. Special thanks are due to researchers Paul Boothe, Michael Charette, and John Gartenburg for a magnificent job done in compiling and processing the data used in this study. Finally, we are indebted to Mrs Jayne Dewar and the typing pool at the University of Western Ontario for their usual fast and efficient service.

SPECULATION AND MONOPOLY IN URBAN
DEVELOPMENT: ANALYTICAL FOUNDATIONS
WITH EVIDENCE FOR TORONTO

1
A guide to the study

INTRODUCTION

The recent period of rapidly rising land and housing prices in major Canadian metropolitan areas[1] has generated considerable public discussion and occasional legislative action. Yet in spite of this response, there do not seem to exist suitable analyses of land markets which attempt to determine the causes of these price increases, and to recommend suitable policy measures. Policies that have been advanced in public debate are sometimes either formulated without attention to underlying causes or are based on assumed causes of questionable theoretical and empirical validity. The first purpose of this study, therefore, is to provide a theoretical analysis of the land development process, the change in land prices over time, and the effects of speculation, monopoly elements, and public policy on land development. The second purpose of the study is to apply this theoretical framework to an empirical analysis of the Toronto land market. Specifically, we will attempt to determine the level of ownership concentration and market power in that market, and attempt to arrive at an understanding of the land assembly process and the role played by speculators in that process.

---

1 The reader is referred to Appendix A for data which document the rise in land and housing prices during the seventies.

4 Speculation and monopoly in urban development

Embodied both in the public discussion and in some of the governmental re-sponse[2] is a notion that the rate of increase and the level of land and housing prices are partly attributable, at least in the short run, to agents called 'specu-lators.' Although this pejorative term is commonly used, it is difficult to find an explicit definition of 'speculator' anywhere in the written record of public discussion.[3] It is equally difficult to ascertain how people think speculators affect the market other than that their actions somehow raise prices. Part of the problem here is the frequent failure to draw a distinction between speculators (who may be competitive agents) and agents with market power[4] (who may or may not engage in speculation). In any case, we seem to be left with the notion that speculators withhold land from final users in hopes of higher prices in the future. Thus speculation is thought to be socially undesirable for two basic reasons. First, speculation is thought to lead to a misallocation of resources through slowing the rate of development and raising prices above their 'ordinary' (perfectly competitive?) levels. Second, speculation is thought to redistribute income from the community at large to the speculators.

One of our first problems in assessing the role of speculation in the land market is to develop a suitable definition of a 'land speculator.' Traditionally, in the economics literature, the term *investor* has been used (although not ex-clusively) for an agent who provides capital which he assumes is to be used in the production of goods and services. The term *speculator* has been used (again, not exclusively) for an agent who buys and sells assets for the purpose of realizing a capital gain. Although some acts of investing could be called speculation and *vice versa*, in some contexts the distinction is clear. Lending money to a firm for the purposes of its buying a capital good is clearly an act of investment. However, trading in foreign exchange markets, for the purpose of realizing a capital gain (as opposed to pure hedging) is clearly an act of speculation. In the spirit of these definitions we will define a speculator in the land market as an agent who buys and sells land without the intention of effecting improvements, or using the land as an input in a production process. We will define an investor in the land market as an agent who purchases land for use as an input in a production process, or is in the business of 'transforming' land (e.g., subdividing and

---

2 The most notable governmental response is the Ontario Land Speculation Tax Act, enacted in April 1974. The structure of this tax along with the motivation behind its introduction will be discussed in chapter 7.

3 Of course the Ontario Land Speculation Tax defines speculation, implicitly, as a trans-action which is subject to the tax.

4 An agent has market power if he can affect *market* prices.

servicing). Notice that under our definition it is possible for an agent to be a speculator in some of his activities and an investor in others.

Although there has been considerable economic literature devoted to the analysis of speculative activity and its effects, none of this literature can be directly applied to the land market. For example, most of the previous literature on speculation has been concerned with foreign exchange and stock markets. The land market differs from these markets in many ways, but perhaps most importantly land, unlike foreign exchange or common shares, is a direct input in the production process of an industry – the development and housing industry. Thus the question as to how speculation in the land market affects the production of serviced land is of a type which is not addressed in the literature on foreign exchange and stock markets. This type of issue is partially dealt with in some of the literature concerned with commodity futures markets, but only at a rudimentary level. However, since there is not a well-defined futures market for land, the commodity futures market literature is not very applicable. Therefore, as part of this study we have had to develop a theoretical model of speculation appropriate for the land market.

MONOPOLY ELEMENTS IN THE LAND MARKET

Another notion that has been continually advanced in Canada is that rapidly rising land prices are due to monopoly elements in the land market. Two studies (Dennis and Fish, 1972; Spurr, 1974, 1976), for example, claim to have documented a high degree of ownership concentration in the Toronto area. Even higher concentration has been claimed for some other Ontario cities. Presumably, monopoly ownership results in the holding of land off the market in order to raise prices. Like speculation, this is thought to slow the rate of land development and to cause an income redistribution in favor of developers relative to a competitive market allocation.

There are, however, a number of theoretical difficulties connected with the notion of monopoly power in urban areas around which there is a virtually infinite hinterland of undeveloped land. A developer who owns 'large' amounts of land close to the urban area may only own a small fraction of all 'available' land depending upon how far from the built-up area one is willing to travel in defining 'available.' It is apparent that land is spatially differentiated, with land close to built-up areas being a superior good to land which lies further away. The meaning of concentration and market power in urban land markets must, therefore, be clarified before the issue of its existence can be properly dealt with empirically.

A second problem is that the effects of market power (however defined) are less clear here than in other types of markets. One example is in order. Like any other land investor, a monopolist owning a fixed stock of land may wish to develop that land within a fixed time horizon (e.g., before retirement age). If this is true, holding some of his land off the market in the present period in order to increase present prices may leave him only with more land to unload in later years at depressed prices. It is not immediately clear, therefore, that the existence of ownership concentration and market power will lead to a slower rate of land development than would prevail under competitive conditions. Therefore, as in the case of an analysis of speculation, we have found it necessary to develop some theoretical models so that the role of monopoly elements in the land market could be analysed.

OUTLINE OF THE THEORETICAL RESEARCH

The theoretical research presented in subsequent chapters concentrates on four topics. The first of these is the question as to whether or not concentration of land ownership confers market power on large landowners, and what the existence of such market power implies for the equilibrium configuration of an urban area. Our research on this topic also clarifies the distinction between Ricardian rents and the returns to market power in the land market, a distinction which is not particularly clear in the existing literature. This material occupies chapter 2 of this study. The second topic of our research is an examination of the land development process, i.e., a theoretical analysis of the determinants of the timing of development and the pattern of land prices over time for different market structures in a world of certainty, and an analysis of the effects of different types of taxation on the development process. These issues are developed in chapter 3.

The third topic concerns the relationship between 'the' return to land speculation and the returns on other risky assets. The last topic is the effects of the existence of uncertainty and speculation on the development process. Suitable analysis of this topic has required us to develop a general equilibrium model incorporating markets for two kinds of land, and the presence of intertemporal uncertainty. This is found in chapter 4.

Our analysis has convinced us that much of the previous literature on land markets has ignored two critical attributes of the land market. First, because of land's inherent durability, static models cannot adequately capture many of the important features of the land market. Second, land is in some of its important characteristics inherently heterogeneous. Thus in assessing the effects of market power on land use, the geographical heterogeneity of land cannot be ignored. Also, 'speculative' land is inherently heterogeneous with respect to risk, so that *the* return to land speculation is not a meaningful concept.

OUTLINE OF THE EMPIRICAL RESEARCH

The theoretical research component of this study is designed to arrive at an understanding of the land development process: the determinants of market power in the land market, the timing and spatial character of land development under competitive versus monopolistic market conditions, and the pattern of land price movements over time. The results provide a basis for an empirical study which can quantify some of the parameters of the theoretical models. This empirical evidence is also of interest because the theory we develop shows that the effects of present and future government policy on land development depend on such things as the existence of market power and the degree of uncertainty.

The Toronto area was chosen to be the basis of our empirical research. This city is particularly interesting (although not necessarily representative) because the very high rate of price appreciation on land has brought charges that monopoly and speculative activity have somehow caused the high prices. Our first empirical section (chapter 5), therefore, is devoted to an analysis of whether or not there is sufficient ownership concentration in undeveloped land around Toronto to suggest the existence of significant market power. The methodology with which this analysis is conducted is based on the theoretical results of chapter 2.

A second set of empirical issues we address is concerned with the process by which land moves from owner-operated farms into land approved for sub-dividing. We are interested in seeing what role speculators (as we have defined them) play in this process, in how long before sub-division do developers begin to assemble land tracts, and actual rates of price appreciation over time. Answers to all these questions will help to quantify the theory models developed in earlier chapters. One motivation is provided by the Ontario Land Speculation Tax which heavily taxes capital gains on land made by speculators but which generally allows actual developers to escape taxation.

REMARKS TO THE READER

Our original purpose in this study was to analyse the role of speculation and monopoly elements in the land market, and the effects of the Ontario Land Speculation Tax on the functioning of the land market. In pursuing this purpose we discovered that the existing literature was deficient in providing answers to some very basic questions. Thus we were led to augment the existing literature with further analysis in order to develop a theory of the land market and development process which would allow us to consider the effects of the presence of speculation and monopoly elements. This has resulted in the study becoming more technical but, we think, more interesting than we originally envisaged.

We believe that our findings should be of interest to a wide range of individuals: academics, policy makers, and more casual readers who wish to understand the recent booms in land and house prices. Our fear, however, is that the technical nature of parts of the analysis may cause some readers to dismiss the study as an academic exercise. We hope that this will not be the case and would emphasize to such readers that some conceptual perspective is necessary both for constructing and for interpreting the results of empirical research. Indeed, chapter 5 (our first empirical section) begins by strongly criticizing some previous empirical work as nonsensical: a situation which resulted from a failure to understand the development process before plunging into the data. Thus we urge readers who are disinterested in theory to first read the summaries found at the end of the theoretical chapters (2, 3, and 4), which indicate the results of academic and policy interest found in these chapters. It is hoped that these summaries will entice the reader to examine the contents of these chapters. An over-all summary of the results of the study and our policy recommendations can be found in chapter 7. Finally, our explanation of the basic causes of the urban real estate boom of the 1970s can be found on pages 54-7.

2

Ownership concentration and market power in urban land markets

INTRODUCTION

As we saw in our introductory chapter, 'monopoly elements' in the land market have been one of the most popular targets in assessing blame for high land prices. Presumably the mechanism thought to be operating here is that large landowners withhold land from the market in order to raise prices. The evidence generally cited for the existence of such monopolistic behaviour is of two types. First it is argued that a small group of large landowners own a major portion of the land suitable for development in many urban areas. Second, the current large spread between the prices of agricultural and urban land is often cited as evidence of market power.[1] In this chapter we will consider a simple model of an urban area which will serve as a framework for analysing the connection between concentrated ownership, the difference between agricultural and urban land prices, and the existence of market power. This model will also allow us to analyse the effects of *exercised* market power on the structure of urban areas.

Our analysis will address the following questions: (1) What is a meaningful concept of concentration in the context of land markets? (2) What is the relationship between concentration and the existence of market power? (3) What is the distinction between Ricardian rents and the return to market power in land markets? (4) What are the allocative effects of *exercised* market power? Before proceeding with our analysis, we will clarify the issues addressed in these four questions, by discussing them briefly in turn.

1 An agent has market power if he can affect market prices.

The first question arises because the land market requires a definition of concentration which is different from those commonly applied to other industries. The usual problem encountered in defining concentration is that of determining a suitable definition of the industry, i.e., deciding which firms are in the industry. For an urban land market the problem is to determine the appropriate universe of land.

Since concentration in an industry does not necessarily imply the existence of market power unless there are significant barriers to entry, deviations in market structure from perfect competition cannot generally be inferred simply on the basis of concentration. As we will see, however, in the market for urban land, concentration itself is a barrier to entry, and so deviation from competition can be inferred on the basis of concentration. The third question is of particular importance since much of the public discussion of land prices seems to misinterpret Ricardian rents as returns to market power. This confusion could lead to serious errors in the choice of appropriate policies. In our analysis of the fourth question we examine the effect of exercised market power on the structure of land prices and on the geographical configuration of the urban area.

THE MODEL

We will use a model of a circular city which is adapted from Solow's version of the standard urban location model (Solow, 1973). Because of its static nature, the model must be interpreted as a long-run equilibrium model. Although this model is an extremely simplified version of reality, we will see that it greatly clarifies some of the important aspects of the urban land market. To simplify our analysis, we will make some very restrictive assumptions. However, in the later section on assumptions we will show that our basic conclusions do not require such restrictions. The technical details of the analysis of the model can be found in appendix B. Since we wish to examine the relationship between concentration, *per se*, and market power, we will assume that there is an arbitrarily large amount of homogeneous land so that there are no 'entry' barriers resulting from limited supplies of specialized land. For simplicity, we will assume that all production activities occur in a Central Business District (CBD), which is a circular region of fixed size with radius R, and we will ignore the production aspect of the CBD other than to assume that a composite consumption good and composite housing good are produced. The consumption good is produced by a perfectly competitive industry at constant costs. The composite housing good, also produced by a perfectly competitive industry, is a flow of housing services consisting of housing and land in fixed proportions, so that the housing composite is measured by lot size. The supply price of a unit of housing services at distance x from the CBD, excluding the cost of land, is $C(x)$, where $C'(x) \geq 0$.[2] Thus $C(x)$ includes the cost of providing and maintaining serviced land and housing at distance x from the CBD, but *not* the (rental) cost of the raw land. With no loss in generality, we assume that land outside the CBD has no economic use other than for housing.

Households thus consume a single composite consumption good and a composite housing good. Each consumer must travel daily to the CBD and incurs an annual transportation cost of $T(x)$ if he lives at distance x from the CBD, with $T'(x) > 0$. For simplicity we assume that the population of the city consists of N identical consumers. We can then summarize each consumer by a utility function $U(c,h)$ (where c measures units of the consumption composite and h measures units of the housing composite), and a budget constraint $c + r(x)h + T(x) = w$ (where $r(x)$ is the *total* rent per unit of the housing composite at distance x from the CBD, and the price of the consumption composite is set equal to one). Although in this chapter we will focus our attention on the rent gradient, assertions about sales prices can easily be made by appropriate capitalization.

The equilibrium rent gradient, $r(x)$, is determined from two conditions. First, since all consumers are identical, in equilibrium they all must attain the same level of utility, i.e., the rent gradient must be such that everyone is indifferent as to where they live. Notice that this condition is independent of the structure of the land market (i.e., whether the land market is perfectly or imperfectly competitive). This then requires that $r'(x) < 0$, i.e., the rent gradient falls with distance from the CBD, because otherwise consumers living further from the CBD could not attain the same utility level as those who live nearer to the CBD. Identical utility levels are possible because the further a consumer lives from the CBD, the more of the housing composite he consumes.

The second condition determining $r(x)$ requires that everyone must live somewhere. The demand for land is determined by the requirement that all consumers attain equal utility. The 'supply' of land is determined by the structure of the land market. The second condition thus requires that the structure be consistent with all consumers being located in equilibrium. This condition is also independent of the structure of the land market. We will now compare equilibria for different market structures in this simple model.

PERFECT COMPETITION

Consistent with perfect competition, we will assume that all land is owned in small parcels by individual landowners. For simplicity we will assume they are

2 The model would allow $C'(x) < 0$, although this could lead to problems of instability of equilibrium.

Figure 1

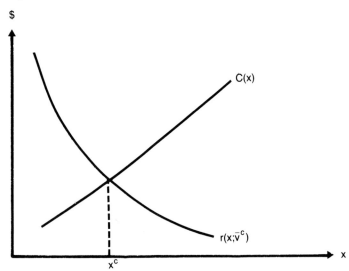

absentee landowners. If the equilibrium rent gradient is $r^c(x)$, then the rent per unit of land accruing to owners of land at x is $r^c(x) - C(x)$ (for land actually occupied). Since we have assumed that the land market is competitive and that the only economic use of land is for housing, if $r^c(x) - C(x) > 0$, then all land at distance x will be supplied in equilibrium. Therefore we can now completely characterize the equilibrium for the competitive city. The competitive equilibrium rent gradient, $r^c(x)$, must satisfy three conditions: (1) all consumers have identical utility; (2) all consumers are located; and (3) the land occupied in equilibrium is all land within distance x^c of the CBD, where x^c is such that $r^c(x^c) = C(x^c)$. Therefore $R + x^c$ is the equilibrium radius of the competitive city.

This equilibrium is depicted in Figure 1. Notice that the vertical distance between $r^c(x)$ and $C(x)$ at any x is the Ricardian rent earned on land at distance x from the city. This premium earned on land because of its location is apparently mistaken in some public discussions for evidence of market power. This is a serious mistake if it leads to policy measures which attempt to change the allocation of land in a situation where the land market is competitive, since the competitive allocation (in the absence of externalities) is efficient, and Ricardian rents are necessary for efficient allocation. However, the question as to who should earn these rents is a distributional matter, which we will not deal with here.

MONOPOLY

For the land market to be a simple monopoly, one landowner must own all the 'available' land. One strong, but reasonable definition of the 'available' land is all land within $\bar{x}$ of the CBD, where $\bar{x}$ is the distance at which transportation costs exhaust income. In this section we assume that one landowner owns all this land, and that his objective is to maximize his total rent.

For any given supply of land the monopolist puts on the market, demand determines the equilibrium rent gradient. Consider for example a potential supply by the monopolist of all land within some distance $\hat{x}$ from the CBD, where $\hat{x} < x^c$. For this supply, the requirements that all consumers have identical utility, and that everyone lives somewhere will determine an equilibrium rent gradient. Now consider reducing this supply by one unit of land. This will have the effect of shifting up the rent gradient at every distance from the CBD. The amount the rent gradient is shifted up depends on where the unit of land is taken from. The reason for this is as follows. The consumption of land per consumer increases with distance from the CBD, and so the density of consumers decreases with distance from the CBD. Therefore one unit of land taken away from near the CBD displaces more consumers who must live elsewhere, than one unit of land near $\hat{x}$. This means that taking a unit of land away shifts up the rent gradient more, the closer the unit is to the CBD.

The key to the monopolist's decision is the number of people who will live at each distance from the CBD. To be consistent with appendix B, let $-\Psi(>0)$ be the reduction in maximized total rent paid if there is one less consumer in the city. The net rent paid by one person living at distance x is $[r(x) - C(x)]h(x)$, where $h(x)$ is the amount of land consumed. As shown in the appendix, the marginal conditions for the monopolist require that for the monopolist to sell land at distance x, it must be the case that $[r(x) - C(x)]h(x) \geqq -\Psi$. Let us now examine this condition in more detail.

Intuition might suggest that the monopolist's marginal conditions would involve setting marginal revenue and marginal cost *per unit of land* equal. This intuition however is incorrect. The reason for this is that from the monopolist's viewpoint land is not his scarce resource but rather the *number of consumers*. Selling land 'uses up' consumers, and the closer the land is to the CBD, the more consumers he 'uses up.' For example, an acre of land near the CBD will be a high-density, high-rise development, in which many consumers will live, while an acre of land near the edge of the city will be a low density, single-family detached development, in which few consumers will live. Therefore the marginal conditions require that the marginal revenue per person at distance

Figure 2

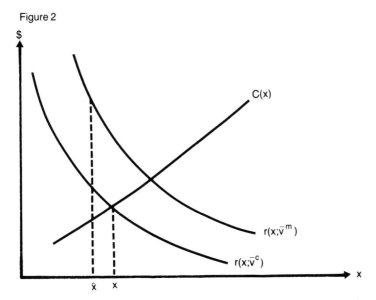

x ($[r(x) - C(x)]h(x)$) exceed the marginal cost per person at x, for him to sell land at distance x.

Not surprisingly, it is shown in the appendix that the monopolist will restrict the supply of land relative to the competitive city, resulting in a uniformly higher rent gradient, lower utility, and higher density. The difference between the monopoly equilibrium rent gradient and the competitive equilibrium rent gradient at any x represents the differential returns to market power, or the monopoly rent, earned at land at distance x.

One surprising result derived in the appendix is that monopoly equilibrium city may have vacant land within the boundaries of occupation, i.e., the monopolist may choose to have leapfrog development.[3] The reason this may occur is that although a unit of land nearer the CBD is more valuable than a unit nearer the edge of the city, withholding the unit near the CBD will raise the rent gradient more than withholding a unit nearer the edge.

In Figure 2, we can compare the competitive rent gradient $r^c(x)$ and the monopoly rent gradient $r^m(x)$. Although this diagram was drawn on the assumption that leapfrogging does not occur, it is of course true that $r^m(x) > r^c(x)$ at each x, independent of whether or not leapfrogging occurs. In the diagram the distinction between Ricardian rent and monopoly rent can be

___

3 Alternative explanations of leapfrogging have been given elsewhere in the literature. For example, see Ohls and Pines (1975).

clearly seen, since $r^c(x) - C(x)$ is the *Ricardian rent* and $r^m(x) - r^c(x)$ is the *monopoly rent* derived on land at distance x from the CBD.

'CONCENTRATED' OWNERSHIP

Of course except for a few historical exceptions, urban land markets are not characterized by monopoly land ownership. Thus where concentration has been a matter of public concern, it has usually been in urban areas in which it is thought that a 'few' large landowners own a 'significant' proportion of the land suitable for development. When accused of artifically raising land prices large landowners have often responded by arguing that there is a considerable amount of topographically similar land in the area which they do not own, and so they are forced to 'compete' just like any small landowner. We might paraphrase this argument by saying that although there may be significant concentration, because of large *potential* supplies there are no significant barriers to entry, at least in the market for topographically similar land.

The crucial flaw in this sort of argument is that land has at least *two* important attributes: topography and distance from employment centres. In a particular urban area there may be an effectively unlimited supply of land of similar topography, but there is necessarily a restricted supply of such land within any fixed commuting time to employment centres, which results in there being a natural entry barrier. Thus, in our model, if one landowner owns all land within distance $\bar{x}$ of CBD, there is an effective absolute entry barrier. The more concentrated is the ownership of land, the higher are the barriers to entry, since the more land a large landowner owns, the smaller is his potential competition. Therefore significant concentration of land ownership is a sufficient condition for the existence of potential market power.

However, it is very important for the reader to be clear as to the appropriate definition of universe of land – i.e., the appropriate definition of the urban residential land *market*. The proper definition of the residential land market for an urban area includes all 'developable' land (within reasonable commuting distance of employment centres), and *all developed residential land*. All developed residential land must be included in the definition of the market since the consumption demand for residential land is always also a joint demand for housing, so that the existing stock of developed land is a very good substitute for vacant lots.

For a small group of large landowners to have potential market power in an (appropriately defined) urban area, two conditions must hold. First they must own a 'significant' proportion of the universe of developed and 'developable' land. It is difficult here to quantify what would constitute a 'significant' proportion. If the large landowners own one-tenth of one per cent of the appropriately defined universe of land, that is certainly an insignificant proportion. If they own fifty per cent, that is certainly a significant proportion. How significant is the proportion held also depends on the elasticity of demand for land. If the demand for land is very elastic, large landowners would have to withhold a considerable amount of land in order to appreciably affect the price. Therefore to have potential market power the large landowners must own a larger proportion of the universe of land, the more elastic is the demand for land. Since large land assemblies are almost certainly to be holdings of *un-developed* land, even if a small group of large landowners owns enough developable land to constitute a significant proportion of all land (developed and undeveloped), they do not necessarily have potential market power. For example, if a single landowner owns *all* the undeveloped land around an urban area, but the urban area is not growing, he has no market power. Therefore the second condition necessary for potential market power to exist is that the urban area grow enough to eventually include the large landowners' holdings of undeveloped land. Therefore the appropriate basis for a measure of concentration of land ownership for an (appropriately defined) urban area is the totality of developed and 'developable' land within the estimated *future* boundaries of the urban area.

In appendix B we consider a simple model in which there is one large landowner, and all other land is competitively held. We show that a large landowner always has *potential* market power, in that he can affect the equilibrium rent gradient, and so misallocate resources by withholding land (assuming he holds a significant proportion of the land within the boundaries of the competitive city). However, it will not be in his interest in all cases to actually withhold land. Under the assumptions of our model, we are able to derive *sufficient* conditions for the existence of a misallocation of resources. If leapfrogging exists in equilibrium, or if the large landowner owns land at the boundary of equilibrium occupancy, then there has been a misallocation of resources.

A DISCUSSION OF THE ASSUMPTIONS OF THE MODEL

The critical assumptions of our model are: (1) land is topographically homogeneous, (2) there is a fixed number of identical consumers, (3) housing and land are consumed in fixed proportions, and (4) all production occurs in the CBD and therefore all consumers must travel to the CBD to work. The advantage of these assumptions is that they imply a well-defined rent gradient with properties which are easily determined.

Let us now consider the effects of relaxing our assumptions. In assuming that land is homogeneous with respect to all attributes other than location we are ignoring the fact that land is heterogeneous with respect to other attributes, and so the price of any particular parcel of land will have as one of its determinants the vector of the attributes of that land. Thus the owner of a parcel of land with particularly 'good' attributes will earn 'large' Ricardian rents. However, he will not earn *monopoly* rents on his parcel unless he has market power and exercises it. Our earlier analysis in this chapter indicates that he will not have market power unless his land holdings are a significant proportion of the totality of 'developable' land in the urban area where 'developability' is a summary statistic of the attributes of land, which includes physical features, serviceability, zoning, and the government approval process. Thus the fact that land is heterogeneous indicates that the amount of 'developable' land in any urban area is smaller than the universe of serviceable land within reasonable commuting distance. However, our basic conclusion that market power can result only from concentrated ownership of 'developable' land (suitably defined) is still valid.

Our assumption that consumers are identical is simply for technical convenience. If we allowed consumers to be different, then it would be more difficult to derive the properties of the equilibrium, but our basic conclusions would still hold. However, the assumption that the number of consumers is fixed is not so innocent. In a world where there was perfect mobility of consumers and production between urban areas, even a monopoly land owner in one urban area would not have market power, since mobility of consumers and production would ensure that land with identical attributes would have a common price in all urban areas. However, it would appear that the majority of producers and consumers are probably not mobile between urban areas which are not in the same general commuting area, at least for the medium run. Therefore we would argue that concentrated land ownership in a particular (suitably defined) urban area does give the large landowners potential market power.

Let us now consider our assumption that land and housing are consumed in fixed proportions. Of course this is not a reasonable assumption, but dispensing with it does not significantly modify our conclusions. If housing and land are not consumed in fixed proportions then the extent of large landowners' potential market power (i.e., the extent to which they can affect land prices) is reduced if the large landowners do not also have market power in the construction industry. This is because higher land prices will cause consumers to economize on land relative to housing, making the derived demand for land more elastic, reducing the potential market power of large landowners.

Our assumption that all production occurs in the CBD was made to ensure that land was homogeneous with respect to all attributes except a single distance measure. If, as in most urban areas, there are significant employment centres outside the CBD, the definition of the urban area appropriate for measures of concentration may not coincide with the entire city, at least in the short run, especially for large cities. For the long run, when production facilities are mobile, the appropriate definition of the urban area is the city. We will discuss the problem in more detail in connection with the empirical results presented in chapter 5.

Although the assumptions of the model developed in this chapter are very unrealistic, we have seen that our basic conclusions will hold with much more realistic assumptions.

SUMMARY AND CONCLUSIONS

In this chapter we showed that concentration in the ownership of land in an urban area is a sufficient condition for the existence of potential market power. The appropriate basis of the measure of concentration for a suitably defined urban area was shown to be the totality of 'developable' and developed (residential) land within the estimated future boundaries of the urban area. We analysed the allocative effects of exercised market power, and the distinction between Ricardian rents and returns to market power was clarified. It was shown that concentrated ownership always confers potential market power on the large landowners and that the existence of leapfrogging, or the fact that large (relative to the appropriate universe of land) landowners own land near the outer boundary of the city may indicate that resources have been misallocated due to exercised market power.

Casual empiricism suggests that the conditions which may imply the existence of resource misallocation are commonly found in many North American areas. Developers of course generally do hold land near the boundary of the city. Leapfrog development also appears to be a fairly common phenomenon. Of course some leapfrogging is simply the result of topography, and thus has nothing to do with market power. In other cases leapfrogging is apparently the result of zoning. However, it may be wrong to attribute such leapfrogging to zoning, since if ownership is concentrated, zoning may largely reflect developers' preferences.

There remains, of course, the empirical question of whether or not concentration exists. Our analysis has shown that this is a question which ought to be answered.

3
The timing of land development

In chapter 2 and appendix B we proved that it was meaningful to discuss market power in the land market, and derived the effects of exercised market power. However, the static model we used for our analysis can give us only limited insights into the working of the land market, since that model depicts the long-run equilibrium of an urban area. It cannot usefully tell us much about the land development process in a growing urban area. In this chapter we will develop a simple intertemporal general equilibrium model of the land market, which will clarify the relationship between the timing of development and market structure. We will also analyse the effects of various government policies on the timing of development and the rate of appreciation of land prices.

The motivation for our analysis is that the land development process is not well understood, since many of our ideas about the land market are borrowed from analyses of other types of markets. These ideas, which often form the foundation of legislative proposals, may be inappropriate for a number of reasons. Unlike housing units or capital goods, for example, the supply of land of given characteristics (e.g., commuting distance to the city centre) is fixed in the long run in any metropolitan area. Any decision to develop land for residential use, therefore, necessarily reduces the total stock of undeveloped land with these characteristics by the amount of land developed. Since land developers' timing of transactions will clearly reflect this fact, any analysis of land pricing ought to be placed in a dynamic framework.

Perhaps the most important difference between the land market and other markets occurs on the demand side. Consumers receive satisfaction from the flow of services derived from the stock of residential land they own. The flow demand for new residential land in any period is best thought of as a stock adjustment demand. Further, there is virtually no depreciation on land. This implies that increased sales of developed land in the current period will, *ceteris paribus*, decrease the demand for new residential land in future periods. A developer must realize that sales of land by competitors in the present period will affect the future demand for, and therefore the value of his holdings.

Although it is generally recognized that the rate of price appreciation is somehow related to the rate of interest, the exact mechanism has never been well specified. The model presented here develops this relationship explicitly and shows how it depends upon development costs, agricultural opportunity costs, and the level of Ricardian rents on land. With Ricardian rents positive, for example, it is shown that it is Ricardian rents on land rather than the price of land that tends to appreciate at the rate of interest.

Of particular interest will be the relationship between market structure, land prices and the timing of land development. We will demonstrate that with land in fixed supply, a monopolist is less likely to develop all his land than a competitive development industry within a given time horizon. If demand is sufficient for a monopolist to develop all his land profitably, however, monopoly generally cannot lead to *both* a slower rate of development and a steeper rate of price appreciation than would occur under conditions of competition. The conditions under which a monopolist will develop land faster than a competitive industry are also presented and interpreted.

Other results include a demonstration that the institution of a property tax or a capital gains tax must reduce the initial period price of developed land in a competitive situation. It is further shown that a capital gains tax will lead to a higher rate of land development and a higher rate of price appreciation than would prevail in the absence of the tax. Questions of tax incidence and the distinction between Ricardian rents and returns to market power are also dealt with.

The model presented here makes a number of simplifying assumptions in order to focus clearly on the intertemporal patterns of land sales and land prices in a general equilibrium framework.[1] First, it is assumed that the total amount of

---

1 Much of the analysis of land markets found in the literature is questionable, due to an attempt to force an inherently general equilibrium problem into a partial equilibrium framework. In some of the models it is assumed that 'demand for land' grows monotonically over time (interpreted to mean an outward shift in Marshallian demand curve) in a way that is most conveniently expressed by a concave function $V(T)$ which gives the value of land holdings at time T (see, for example, Bahl, 1968; Shoup, 1969). This approach assumes away all interesting aspects of the problem and guarantees a number of results *a priori*. For example, the (unjustified) assumption that $V(T)$ is strictly concave

undeveloped land available to the city for future residential construction is fixed over the relevant time horizon. Given our analysis in chapter 2 and appendix B, we should consider this land to be the stock of developable land within reasonable commuting time of the employment centres of this urban area. Second, it is assumed that this fixed land stock is homogeneous topographically, and we will ignore the spatial distribution of land. These assumptions simplify considerably the mathematical complexity of the model, without sacrificing the applicability of the insights gained from our analysis.

DEMAND FOR RESIDENTIAL LAND

Let us begin by constructing a two-period model in which a fixed stock of land, initially held by a group referred to as developers, is prepared for residential construction and sold to consumers over the course of two time periods.[2] In this chapter we will assume that there is perfect certainty, so that everyone knows both this period's prices and next period's prices. Of course there is no forward market, as such, in the land market, so we must clarify how the model is to be interpreted. In a steadily growing urban area which is in long-run equilibrium, we would expect that developers and consumers would be able to predict future prices with considerable accuracy. Our model presented in this chapter should therefore be interpreted as a long-run equilibrium model of a growing urban area. For example, we would expect that the model could quite reasonably be applied to the Toronto area during the sixties. However, the short-run dynamics of the land market in some circumstances will depend crucially on the uncertainty faced by agents in the land market, and their reaction to this uncertainty. The important addition of uncertainty and speculation to the analysis is left for chapter 4.

It is perhaps conceptually useful to think of the two periods in our model as being the present and future, and therefore the periods are not necessarily of equal length. Our analysis could be fairly easily extended to a many-period framework, but only with a serious loss of clarity of exposition, so in this

ensures us that the institution of the property tax will reduce the otpimal length of time that an investor will hold land. For one attempt to actually explain the equilibrium increase in valuation over time, see Bentick (1972).

2 For the purposes of this paper, the assumption of two periods is important in that it assumes a fixed time horizon but not in that it assumes only two periods. All conclusions will be essentially valid in a multi-period model. Also, it should be noted that landowners may sell land among themselves as may consumers. Any sale by a landowner to a consumer, however, is assumed to be irreversible.

chapter we will restrict ourselves to a two-period model. In chapter 4 we consider a multi-period model. Developers may perform servicing functions such as subdivision, sewer installation, and road building, so serviced land will be referred to as developed land. It is assumed that consumers have no alternative sources of land and that consumers contract for housing construction once they have purchased land.[3] The purpose of this assumption is to keep a clear distinction between land and housing prices, the former being the focus of this chapter.

Let us first consider the determinants and properties of the demand for land of an individual consumer. If we conceive of our model as a small community in the middle of a large free-trade region, we can assume that all commodities are traded with the region and the commodity prices to the small community are fixed. These prices are then independent of the price of land, the distribution of income, etc. Various types of housing units that consumers can construct on their land are numbered among these commodities. The assumption that commodity prices are fixed to the community allows us to make use of the composite commodity theorem to aggregate all other commodities into a single composite commodity and to express preferences as a function of the composite commodity and the stock of land held by the consumer.[4] Denoting the composite commodity purchased in time T as C_T and the purchase of land in time T as L_T, the consumer's two-period utility function is given by:

$$U = U_0(C_0, L_0) + U_1(C_1, L_0 + L_1), \tag{1}$$

where U_i gives the present value of the flow of utility at $T = i$ and where U_i is assumed to have the usual quasi-concave properties. Additivity is assumed only for the convenience of graphical exposition. $(L_0 + L_1)$ appears as an argument in U_1 since utility at time $T = 1$ is derived from the total amount of land owned by the consumer and not just from land purchased at $T = 1$. It is important to remember in what follows that L_1 is the *incremental* demand for land in period 1. A final assumption of this formulation is that land does not depreciate physically.

3 Although this assumption is admittedly unrealistic, it is true that the building and development industries are often quite separate. In Toronto, for example, few developers have building divisions of any consequence. The building industry includes a great many small companies, most of whom buy serviced building lots for immediate construction. Further, total holdings of undeveloped land by individuals and builders is small compared with holdings by development companies.

4 The purpose of this assumption is to reduce the general equilibrium model to the problem of determining a single relative price.

The composite commodity is used as numeraire and community income in period T in terms of C_T is denoted Y_T,[5] where Y_T is known with certainty, and p_T will denote the price of land in period T in terms of C_T.

The consumer makes consumption plans for both periods by maximizing his two-period utility function subject to a budget constraint that discounts future income and expenditures at a rate i. This rate may be an actual mortgage rate or it may include an added premium for risk.[6] In either case, the budget constraint allows the consumer to borrow or lend subject only to the condition that the present value of the income stream equal the present value of the expenditure stream.

Our discussion of the demand functions of an individual consumer in appendix C leads us to specify *market* demand functions of the form

$$L_0 = D_0(p_0, p_1, \underline{Y}_0, \underline{Y}_1, i)$$
$$L_1 = D_1(p_0, p_1, \underline{Y}_0, \underline{Y}_1, i) \tag{2}$$

where $\underline{Y}_T$ is the vector of incomes of consumers at time T. Assuming that both C_i and L_i are normal goods, $(\partial D_i / \partial p_i) < 0$. The properties of these demand functions are discussed in more detail in appendix C. It is sufficient to note here that for the remainder of the book two additional properties of these demand functions are assumed to hold. First, it is assumed that an increase in the price of land in either period diminishes the total two-period demand for land. In other words, $\partial(L_0 + L_1) / \partial p_i < 0$, for $i = 0, 1$. What is ruled out is the possibility that an increase in p_0, for example, will lead to an increase in L_1 that outweighs the decrease in L_0. Although this seems to be a reasonable assumption, it is not implied by our previous assumptions. Second, we assume that land in different periods is a gross substitute, i.e., $\partial D_i / \partial p_j > 0, i \neq j$.

SUPPLY BY DEVELOPERS – PERFECT COMPETITION

Developers in this urban area own an amount of land, $\bar{L}$, which is assumed to encompass the totality of 'developable' land. This group of 'developers' should be interpreted as the integrated supply side of the urban land market,

---

5 This model is concerned with the determination of relative prices. Changes in nominal prices are found by multiplying through equation (2) in each period by a price index.
6 Of course, if p_1 is an expected price (a random variable) then plans made at the beginning of the initial period must be revised when the actual price is observed in the second period.

encompassing farmers, other landowners, and developers. A more disaggregated model of the development process is developed in chapter 4. In this section we assume that each developer owns only a small amount of $\bar{L}$, so that developers can be assumed to be price takers. The prices of developed land at time zero and one, p_0 and p_1, again are assumed to be known with certainty.

In each period a developer can develop and sell any part of his holdings. For simplicity, the costs of development per unit of land are assumed to be constant and identical in each period, and will be denoted by s. This constant is used to represent such costs as lot servicing and subdivision approval. Land not developed in period one can be rented for agricultural use at a rate denoted by q. Land not developed in the second or 'future' period can earn a stream of returns in agricultural use equal to v ($v \gg q$ assuming the 'future' period is of considerably greater length than the present period). Alternatively, we can assume that land not developed at the beginning of period two is sold for a price equal to v so that developers divest themselves of all land holdings in period two. In this formulation, the relationship $q = rv$ should hold for equilibrium in the market for agricultural land assuming that, for example, the second period was open-ended (again, we have $q \ll v$). Land which is developed during a particular period does not earn any return from agricultural use.

The rate of return on assets judged by developers to be equivalent to land will be denoted by r. The supply of land in each period can now be described as the solution of the problem

$$\max_{L_0, L_1} \quad p_0 L_0 + p_1(1+r)^{-1} L_1 - s L_0 - s(1+r)^{-1} L_1$$
$$+ q(\bar{L} - L_0) + v(1+r)^{-1}(\bar{L} - L_0 - L_1), \tag{3}$$

$$\text{s.t.} \ L_0 + L_1 - \bar{L} \leq 0; L_0, L_1 \geq 0.$$

The restrictions that L_0, $L_1 \geq 0$ amount to the assumption that land development is irreversible. The first order conditions for a maximum are

$$\partial/\partial L_0 = p_0 - s - q - v(1+r)^{-1} - \lambda \leq 0, \tag{4}$$

$$\partial/\partial L_1 = (1+r)^{-1}[p_1 - s - v] - \lambda \leq 0,$$

$$L_0 + L_1 - \bar{L} \leq 0,$$

where λ is the Lagrangean multiplier associated with the constraint on developable land, with $\lambda \geq 0$.

The first order conditions require that a necessary condition for land to be developed in period i, is that the present value of land developed net of development costs, $\Sigma(p_i - s_i)(1 + r)^{-i}$, must be at least as large as the present value of the land in agricultural use, $q + v(1 + r)^{-1}$. If $\lambda > 0$, then all land is sold over the course of the two periods and λ can be interpreted as the Ricardian rent required for land to be sold at time zero. In this case (4) can be interpreted as requiring that Ricardian rents (not land prices) appreciate at rate r for land to be supplied in each period. Notice that even if all land is not sold in period zero, the land sold in that period can still earn positive Ricardian rents. This result is contrary to the usual analysis of Ricardian rents in static models, where the Ricardian factor can earn only positive rents if demand calls for the total supply. This is another indication of the inappropriateness of using static models to analyse the development process.

The equations in (4) leave us with a number of possibilities: (a) that both of the first two equations are less than zero so that no land is developed, (b) the first equation equals zero but the second is less than zero, (c) the second equation equals zero but the first is less than zero, and (d) both equations hold with equality. The last three possibilities give us the following supply characteristics:

$$(L_0, L_1) = \begin{cases} (L_0 > 0, 0), \text{ if } p_0 - p_1(1 + r)^{-1} > q + [s - s(1 + r)^{-1}] \\ (0, L_1 > 0), \text{ if } p_0 - p_1(1 + r)^{-1} < q + [s - s(1 + r)^{-1}] \\ (L_0 > 0, L_1 > 0), \text{ if } p_0 - p_1(1 + r)^{-1} = q + [s - s(1 + r)^{-1}]. \end{cases} \quad (5a)$$

This can also be written

$$(L_0, L_1) = \begin{cases} (L_0 > 0, 0), \text{ if } (p_1 - p_0)/p_0 < r - [q(1 + r) + sr]/p_0 \\ (0, L_1 > 0), \text{ if } (p_1 - p_0)/p_0 > r - [q(1 + r) + sr]/p_0 \\ (L_0 > 0, L_1 > 0), \text{ if } (p_1 - p_0)/p_0 = r - [q(1 + r) + sr]/p_0 \end{cases} \quad (5b)$$

If, in addition, the third equation of (4) holds such that all land is developed and $\lambda > 0$, then $L_0 + L_1$ in (5a) and (5b) must equal $\bar{L}$. In this case, (4) requires that the Ricardian rent at time zero, λ, must grow at rate r for land sold in each period.

The interpretation of (5a) and (5b) is straightforward regardless of whether $\lambda = 0$ or $\lambda > 0$. If some land is sold in each period then the rate of price appreciation must be less than r, with the equilibrium rate of price appreciation being an increasing function of p_0, or equivalently, of λ. Alternatively, developers will be indifferent to sales in the two periods if the difference between the present price of developed land (p_0) and the present value of future price ($p_1 (1 + r)^{-1}$) is just equal to the agricultural revenue foregone by developing at $T = 0$ instead of $T = 1(q)$ plus the burden of incurring development costs at $T = 0$ rather than at $T = 1$ $(s - s(1 + r)^{-1})$.

Notice that in an equilibrium where land is sold in each period, the price of land may fall ($P_1 < P_o$) if λ is in the neighborhood of 0. This is explained by the fact that although equilibrium requires Ricardian rents to appreciate, since the present value of agricultural production at $T = 1$ is less than the present value of agricultural production at $T = 0$, developers may not develop at $T = 0$ unless p_0 exceeds p_1. However, the rate of change of prices is algebraically larger the higher the price of developed land (p_0) relative to the yearly return from agriculture (q). As developed land becomes more and more valuable, positive land sales in each period require a positive rate of price appreciation approaching r, the rate of return on equivalent assets. Similarly, as the length of the second period increases relative to the first, q becomes small relative to v which in turn must be less than $p_1 (q \ll v < p_1)$ if some land is developed in each period. This reduces the difference between the present value of agricultural production at $T = 0$ and $T = 1$ and thus reduces the possibility of a price fall.

MARKET EQUILIBRIUM

Since developed land typically commands a price above its opportunity cost in agriculture in urban areas, for the remainder of this chapter we shall focus on the case where $\lambda > 0$ and all land is developed over the two periods. Given this assumption, the following conditions will characterize equilibrium in the land market:

$$D_0 = S_0; \quad D_1 = S_1; \quad D_0 + D_1 = S_0 + S_1 = \bar{L}; \tag{6}$$

where S_i denotes market supply in period i. Assuming positive sales in each period for the moment, we also have the supply condition:

$$p_0 = p_1(1 + r)^{-1} + q + [s - s(1 + r)^{-1}], \tag{7}$$

$$p_1 = p_0(1 + r) - q(1 + r) - rs.$$

For fixed values of Y_i, we can use equation (2) to write our equilibrium condition as follows:

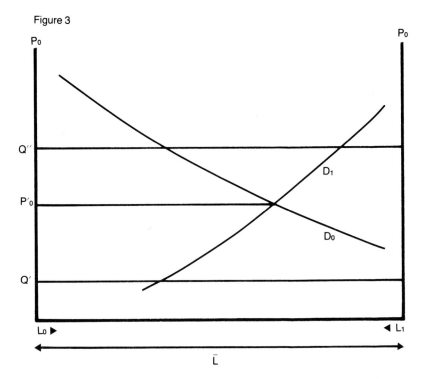

Figure 3

$$D_0(p_0,p_0(1+r) - q(1+r) - rs) + D_1(p_0,p_0(1+r) - q(1+r) - rs) = \bar{L} \quad (8)$$

Equation (8) reduces the equilibrium conditions to a single equation in one unknown (p_0).

A graphical representation of equation (8) is given in Figure 3, where D_0 and D_1 are the first and second period demand curves. We have assumed that a rise in either p_0 or p_1 will, *ceteris paribus*, cause a decrease in the total demand for $L(\partial(L_0 + L_1)/\partial p_i < 0)$. But equation (7) shows that positive land sales in each period require that p_1 be an increasing linear function of p_0. It follows, therefore, that the total excess demand for land must decrease as p_0 increases. This condition is satisfied in Figure 3 where both D_0 and D_1 decrease as p_0 (and therefore p_1) increases. Equilibrium will be at the intersection of D_0 and D_1 provided that $Q = q + v(1+r)^{-1} + s$, representing total opportunity costs, is less than the value of p_0 at this intersection. $Q = Q'$ in Figure 3 provides an example. If $Q = Q''$ in Figure 3, not all of $\bar{L}$ will be developed and the equilibrium values of L_0 and L_1 will be given by the respective intersections of D_0 and D_1 with Q''.

The solution shown in Figure 3 is not the only possibility that satisfies the requirement that increases in p_0 and p_1 reduce total excess demand. D_0 may be upward sloping provided that its slope is less than the absolute value of the slope of D_1. Similarly, D_1 may slope upward provided that its slope is less than the absolute value of the slope of D_0. These conditions are required by our assumption $d(L_0 + L_1) / dp_i < 0$, since:

$$dD_0(p_0, p_0(1 + r) - q(1 + r) - rs) / dp_0 + dD_1(p_0, p_0(1 + r)$$
$$- q(1 + r) - rs) / dp_0$$

$$= [D_{00} + D_{10}] + (1 + r) [D_{01} + D_{11}]$$

$$= d(L_0 + L_1) / dp_0 + (1 + r)d(L_0 + L_1) / dp_1 < 0.$$

A final possibility is that the two demand curves do not cross. If D_i is the upper curve, a corner solution at $L_i = \bar{L}$ will occur provided that the corresponding price exceeds Q. If the corresponding price is less than Q, equilibrium will occur at the value of L_i where $p_0 = Q$.

TAXATION AND MARKET EQUILIBRIUM – PERFECT COMPETITION

We will now consider the effect of two different types of taxes on the competitive equilibrium. First consider the effect of a property tax, assessed at an *ad valorem* rate τ. We assume that developers are taxed on the undeveloped value of their holdings, which we will assume equals $(p_i - s)$ at the beginning of each period. Therefore competitive supply is given as the solution of

$$\max_{L_0, L_1} \quad p_0 L_0 + p_1 (1 + r)^{-1} L_1 - \tau(p_0 - s) \bar{L}$$
$$- \tau(p_1 - s)(1 + r)^{-1} (\bar{L} - L_0) - sL_0 - s(1 + r)^{-1} L_1$$
$$+ q(\bar{L} - L_0) + v(1 + r)^{-1} (\bar{L} - L_0 - L_1), \tag{9}$$
$$\text{subject to } L_0 + L_1 - \bar{L} \leqq 0; L_0, L_1 \geqq 0.$$

Assuming that demand is sufficient for all land to be developed and for some land to be developed in each period, the first order conditions require

$$p_0 - p_1(1 + r)^{-1} (1 - \tau) = q + [s - s(1 + r)^{-1} (1 - \tau)]. \tag{10}$$

The first order conditions for (9) (assuming land is supplied in each period) can also be written

$$(p_1 - p_0)/p_0 = r + \tau p_1/p_0 - [q(1 + r) + s(r + \tau)]/p_0. \tag{11}$$

Letting $[(p_1 - p_0)/p_0]^*$ be the equilibrium rate of price appreciation for $\tau = 0$, and $[(p_1 - p_0)/p_0]^{**}$ be the corresponding rate for $\tau > 0$, (12) can be written

$$(p_1 - p_0)/p_0 \;^{**} = (p_1 - p_0)/p_0 \;^* + \tau(p_1 - s)/p_0, \tag{12}$$

so that the imposition of a property tax increases the equilibrium rate of price appreciation.

We assume that consumers must pay property tax at $T = 1$ on the developed value (at $T = 1$) of land purchased at $T = 0$. Therefore the discounted value of their property tax payments is $\tau p_1(1 + r)^{-1} L_0$. This tax then has the effect of changing the consumer's price of L_0 from p_0 to $p_0 + \tau p_1(1 + r)^{-1}$. Therefore $D_i = D_i(p_0 + \tau p_1(1 + r)^{-1}, p_1)$. For demand to be sufficient for all land to be developed we must have

$$D_0(p_0 + \tau p_1(1 + r)^{-1}, p_1) + D_1(p_0 + \tau p_1(1 + r)^{-1}, p_1) = \bar{L}. \tag{13}$$

Given the assumption that a rise in p_i, ceteris paribus, reduces the total two-period demand for land $(D_{ii} + D_{ji} < 0)$, in appendix D we show that both p_0 and p_1 will fall with the imposition of the tax. Thus the property tax reduces land prices in both periods. We would expect that this would result in a higher equilibrium value for L_0 and a lower value for L_1 than would occur in the absence of the tax. However, since p_0 and p_1 both fall, the effect on equilibrium supplies is ambiguous.[7]

Next, we can consider a tax on realized capital gains which is a simplified version of the original form of the Ontario Land Speculation Tax.[8] Assume that the value of land sales in period $T = 1$ in excess of the value of that land had it been sold in period $T = 0$ is subject to an ad valorem rate of the tax θ. Since development costs are constant, the developed price may be used as a base. Competitive supply is then given by the solution of the following problem:

---

7 It should also be noted that the change in initial period land price in response to the property tax relates to a number of discussions concerning capitalization of the property tax. See, for example, Oates (1969). It should also be noted that government involvement of any sort in the land market creates another form of uncertainty in that government policy is subject to frequent and arbitrary changes. This issue has been raised by Bahl (1968).

8 In its amended form, the Ontario Land Speculation Tax is not assessed on land which has been suitably developed since its purchase. We consider the effects of the Tax in its amended form in chapters 4 and 7.

$$\max_{L_0, L_1} \quad p_0 L_0 + p_1(1+r)^{-1} L_1 - \theta(p_1 - p_0)(1+r)^{-1} L_1 - sL_0$$
$$- s(1+r)^{-1} L_1 + q(\bar{L} - L_0)$$
$$+ v(1+r)^{-1}(\bar{L} - L_0 - L_1), \tag{14}$$
$$\text{such that } L_0 + L_1 - \bar{L} \le 0; L_0, L_1 \ge 0,$$

where we restrict our treatment to the case where $p_1 > p_0$. Assuming land is supplied in each period, the first order necessary conditions for an interior maximum give:

$$p_0(1 - \theta(1+r)^{-1}) - p_1(1+r)^{-1}(1-\theta) = q + (s - s(1+r)^{-1})$$

or

$$(p_1 - p_0)/p_0 = r - [q(1+r) + sr]/p_0(1-\theta). \tag{15}$$

We can also write the second equation of (15) as

$$(p_1 - p_0)/p_0 ^{**} = (1-\theta)^{-1} (p_1 - p_0)/p_0 ^{*}, \tag{16}$$

(where $[(p_1 - p_0)/p_0]^*$ is the equilibrium rate of price appreciation for $\theta = 0$) so that the tax increases the equilibrium rate of price appreciation.

Again assuming that $D_{ii} + D_{ji} < 0$, we show in appendix D that p_0 falls and p_1 rises with the imposition of the tax. Since we have assumed that $D_{ij} > 0$ $(i \neq j)$, it is easily seen that the rate of development is increased by the tax $(dL_0 / d\theta > 0$ and $dL_1 / d\theta < 0)$. The conclusion here is that, with a fixed stock of land that is to be developed within a given time horizon, a capital gains tax will speed the conversion of undeveloped land into final use. Coincident with this higher rate of development, will be a higher rate of increase in the price of land over time than would occur in the absence of these taxes. If the assumptions of this model are a reasonable description of reality, government policymakers cannot hope to use this tax instrument to simultaneously reduce the rate of increase in land prices and speed development. The tax can simultaneously reduce current prices and speed development but only at the expense of making future prices higher.

One final point worth noting concerns the incidence of these taxes. The usual result in a situation where a commodity is in completely inelastic supply is that the supplier bears all of the tax. This is not generally true in this model, since the intertemporal pattern of supply is altered even though total supply remains constant. The present value of consumer payments for $\bar{L}$ (equal to

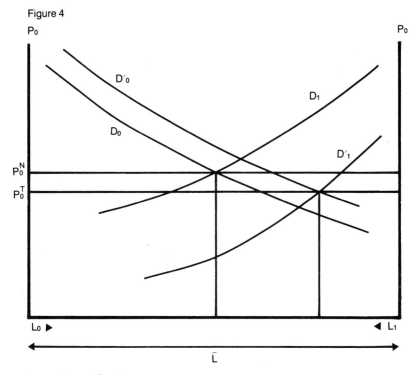

Figure 4

$p_0 L_0 + p_1 (1 + i)^{-1} L_1)$ may either increase or decrease following the taxes depending upon the distribution of purchases between $T = 0$ and $T = 1$ and the change in the equilibrium price ratio, p_1 / p_0.

One possible situation for the capital gains tax is shown graphically in Figure 4 where D_i and D_i' are, respectively, the before and after tax demand curves for period i. p_0^N and p_0^T denote the before and after tax equilibrium prices. The producer equilibrium condition (15) for positive land sales in each period requires that p_1 increase for every value of p_0. Assuming that L_1 is a normal good, D_1 must decrease at every p_0 as shown in Figure 4. Assuming L_0 and L_1 are gross substitutes, D_0 will increase at every p_0. Because $\partial (L_0 + L_1) / \partial p_1 < 0$, the diagram must be as shown with $p_0^T < p_0^N$.

As a final point, note that this tax on realized capital gains cannot cause a reduction in total land developed. The reason for this is given in equations (4), (5a), and (5b), which show that the equilibrium rate of price appreciation becomes negative before the equilibrium value of λ reaches 0. Since non-negative capital gains imply that all land is developed (capital gains occur on Ricardian rents only), the tax cannot be effective in reducing *total* land development.

MONOPOLY AND MARKET EQUILIBRIUM[9]

As suggested earlier in this chapter, there seems to be a common notion that conditions of monopoly generally lead to a smaller supply and a higher price for the commodity in question. This section will investigate the rate of land sales to final users and the path of price increases over time under monopoly and compare the results to the competitive equilibrium described earlier.

With incomes fixed, the demand functions in (2) can be expressed in inverse form by

$$p_0 = p_0(L_0, L_1), \tag{17}$$

$$p_1 = p_1(L_0, L_1).$$

It follows from our earlier assumption that $\partial p_i / \partial L_j > 0$ for $i \neq j$.

Profit maximizing sales by the monopolist are given as the solution of:

$$\begin{aligned}
\underset{L_0, L_1}{\text{Max}} \quad & p_0(L_0, L_1)L_0 + p_1(L_0, L_1)(1 + r)^{-1}L_1 - sL_0 - s(1 + r)^{-1}L_1 \\
& + q(\bar{L} - L_0) + v(1 + r)^{-1}(\bar{L} - L_0 - L_1), \tag{18} \\
& \text{subject to } L_0 + L_1 - \bar{L} \leq 0; L_0, L_1 \geq 0.
\end{aligned}$$

If we define the marginal revenue of land sales in period i as the change in the present value (evaluated at $T = i$) of total revenue with respect to the change in L_i, the first order conditions for (18) can be expressed:

$$\begin{aligned}
MR_0 & = p_0 + (\partial p_0 / \partial L_0) L_0 + (\partial p_1 / \partial L_0)(1 + r)^{-1}L_1 \tag{19} \\
& = p_0 [1 + (1 / \eta_{00}) + (1 + r)^{-1} (R_1 / R_0)(1 / \eta_{01})] \leq s \\
& + q + v(1 + r)^{-1} + \mu;
\end{aligned}$$

9 As in any discussion of monopoly, the analysis and conclusions developed in this section are applicable in oligopolistic situations if the landowner in question either behaves in a Cournot fashion or has fixed expectations about the reactions of other landowners to his sales behaviour. With more sophisticated behaviour, a game theoretic approach is needed.

$$MR_1 = p_1 + (\partial p_1 / \partial L_1) L_1 + (1 + r)(\partial p_0 / \partial L_1) L_0$$

$$= p_1 [1 + (1 / \eta_{11}) + (1 + r)(R_0 / R_1)(1 / \eta_{10})] \leqslant s + v + \mu,$$

where R_i is total sales revenue in period i ($R_i = p_i L_i$), and n_{ij} is the elasticity of demand in period i with respect to p_j, and μ is the Lagrangean multiplier associated with the constraint on developable land, with $\mu \geq 0$.

One important result that follows from the first order conditions is that the monopolist is less likely than the competitor to develop all the land. The competitor will be willing to develop if the developed land price less development costs equals the agricultural opportunity costs. The monopolist will not be willing to develop where marginal revenue less development costs equals the agricultural opportunity cost. Since the average (over $T = 0,1$) marginal revenue earned by land must be less than average price, there must be levels of demand for which the competitive industry will develop all the land, but for which the monopolist will not. Technically, there will be levels of demand for which $\mu = 0$ (marginal rents) in (19) and $\lambda > 0$ (average rents) in (4), the competitive case. In such a case, the monopoly price in each period may exceed the corresponding price under competitive conditions.

As in the competitive case, let us assume that demand is sufficient for some land to be developed in at least one of the two periods. The solution to (18) can then be characterized by the following relationships:

$$(L_0, L_1) = \begin{cases} (L_0 > 0, 0), \text{ if } MR_0 - MR_1(1 + r)^{-1} > q + [s - s(1 + r)^{-1}] \\ (0, L_1 > 0), \text{ if } MR_0 - MR_1(1 + r)^{-1} < q + [s - s(1 + r)^{-1}] \quad (20) \\ (L_0 > 0, L_1 > 0), \text{ if } MR_0 - MR_1(1 + r)^{-1} = q + [s - s(1 + r)^{-1}]. \end{cases}$$

If, in addition, $\mu > 0$ in (18), then $L_0 + L_1$ must equal $\bar{L}$. The expressions in (20) are the same as those in (5a), except that prices have been replaced by marginal revenues.

The situation in which the monopolist chooses to develop all his land is of special interest. Earlier results have demonstrated that the difference between p_0 and p_1 determines directly the equilibrium pattern of supply in that situation. Assuming that some land is supplied in each period, the last equations of (20) and (5a) provide an explicit comparison of the equilibrium prices under the two market structures. Letting p_i^C denote equilibrium market price in period i under competition, and p_i^M the corresponding price under monopoly, subtracting the conditions for positive supplies in each period in (20) (using (19)) from the equivalent expression in (5a), we have:

$$(p^C_0 - p^M_0) - (p^C_1 - p^M_1)(1 + r)^{-1} \tag{21}$$
$$= p^M_0 [(1 / \eta_{00}) + (1 + r)^{-1}(R_1 / R_0) (1 / \eta_{01})] - p^M_1 (1 + r)^{-1}$$
$$[(1 / \eta_{11}) + (1 + r) (R_0 / R_1) (1 / \eta_{10})].$$

Since $d(L_0 + L_1) / dp_i < 0$ by assumption, if all land is developed under both competition and monopoly, then $(p^C_0 - p^M_0)(p^C_1 - p^M_1) < 0$, and $(L^C_0 - L^M_0)$ $(L^C_1 - L^M_1) < 0$. This is because if the price in *each* period was higher under monopoly, total demand would be less than $\bar{L}$. In other words, if the monopoly price at $T = 1$ exceeds the competitive price in the same period, then the monopoly price in $T = 0$ must be less than the corresponding competitive price if total two-period demand is to equal $\bar{L}$ in each case. In such a situation, monopoly will lead to a faster rate of land development and a faster rate of price appreciation than would result under competition. Assuming that the bracketed elasticity expressions in (21) are negative (i.e., that marginal revenue as defined here is less than price in each period), the general result is:

$$\frac{p^M_0 [(1 / \eta_{00}) + (1 + r)^{-1} (R_1 / R_0) (1 / \eta_{01})]}{p^M_1 (1 + r)^{-1} [(1 / \eta_{11}) + (1 + r) (R_0 / R_1) (1 / \eta_{10})]}$$

$$\begin{aligned} &< 1, p^C_0 > p^M_0, L^C_0 < L^M_0 \\ &> 1, p^C_0 < p^M_0, L^C_0 > L^M_0 \\ &= 1, p^C_0 = p^M_0, L^C_0 = L^M_0. \end{aligned} \tag{22}$$

Under fairly general sets of assumptions, there seems to be no reason for believing that this term would be either greater or less than one. The conclusion of this section, therefore, is that, with a fixed stock of land to be developed within a given time horizon, a monopolist may or may not develop land faster than a perfect competition industry depending upon the relevant elasticities given above. This is explained by the fact that the rate of supply and the rate of price increase work in opposite directions. The optimal trade off between these two depends on these demand elasticities. The only thing we can be certain about is that, unless (22) equals 1, equilibrium prices, rate of price appreciation, and rate of development will be different from the competitive equilibrium. Thus unless (22) equals 1, resources will be misallocated. It is possible, however, that demand conditions exist such that (22) equals 1, implying that the competitive and monopoly solutions are identical. In this case although the monopolist still has market power, he does not find it profitable to exercise it.

Notice that except in the unusual case that the monopoly and competitive solutions are identical, in one period monopoly profits will necessarily be smaller than the corresponding competitive Ricardian rents! This shows one of many reasons why it would be incorrect to attempt to verify the existence of exercised market power by measuring the profits of large landowners in a single period (there are, of course, other reasons such as temporary disequilibrium). If competitive prices were known, the difference between the present value of the monopolist's profits and the present value of Ricardian rents would measure the present value of the returns to market power.

In appendix E we present a simple analytic example which compares competitive and monopoly development for linear demand functions.

TAXATION AND MARKET EQUILIBRIUM – MONOPOLY

The effects of property and capital gains taxes under monopoly conditions will be treated very briefly since these effects depend on demand conditions. The monopolist's problem in the case of the property tax is stated as follows:

$$
\begin{aligned}
\text{Max} \atop \{L_0, L_1\} \quad & p_0 L_0 + p_1 (1+r)^{-1} L_1 - \tau(p_0 - s)(L_0 + L_1) \\
& - \tau(p_1(1+r)^{-1} - s(1+r)^{-1}) L_1 - sL_0 - s(1+r)^{-1} L_1 \\
& + q(\bar{L} - L_0) + v(1+r)^{-1}(\bar{L} - L_0 - L_1), \quad (23)
\end{aligned}
$$

such that $L_0 + L_1 - \bar{L} \leq 0$; $L_0, L_1 \geq 0$; $p_0 = p_0(L_0, L_1)$;

$$p_1 = p_1(L_0, L_1).$$

If demand is such that all land is developed and some land is developed in each period, the first order necessary conditions for a maximum give us the following:

$$MR_0{}^* - MR_1{}^* (1+r)^{-1} (1-\tau) = q + [s - s(1+r)^{-1} (1-\tau)] \quad (24)$$

$$
\begin{aligned}
MR_0{}^* = p_0 \, [1 &+ (1-\tau)(1 + (L_1/L_0))(1/\eta_{00}) \\
&+ (1+\tau)(1+r)^{-1} (R_1/R_0)(1/\eta_{01})]
\end{aligned}
$$

$$MR_1{}^* = p_1 \left\{ 1 + (1/\eta_{11}) + [(1+r)(R_0/R_1) - \tau/(1-\tau)](1/\eta_{10}) \right\}.$$

In the case of the capital gains tax, the monopolist's problem is given as follows:

$$\underset{\{L_0, L_1\}}{\text{Max}} \quad p_0 L_0 + p_1(1+r)^{-1} L_1 - \theta(p_1 - p_0)(1+r)^{-1} L_1 - sL_0$$
$$- s(1+r)^{-1} L_1 + q(\bar{L} - L_0) + v(1+r)^{-1} (\bar{L} - L_0 - L_1). \quad (25)$$

Assuming again that all land is developed and some land is developed in each period, the first order necessary conditions give us the following:

$$MR_0' (1 + \theta(1+r)^{-1}) - MR_1' (1+r)^{-1} (1 - \theta) = q + (s - s(1+r)^{-1}); \quad (26)$$
$$MR_0' = p_0 \{1 + (1 - \theta(1+r)^{-1})^{-1} [(1/\eta_{00}) + (R_1/R_0)(1/\eta_{01})]\}$$
$$MR_1' = p_1 \{1 + (1/\eta_{11}) + (1+\theta)^{-1}[(1+r)(R_0/R_1)$$
$$+ \theta(p_0/p_1)](1/\eta_{10})\} .$$

The rate of price appreciation and the pattern of land development resulting from the institution of these taxes in the monopoly case cannot be compared to the no tax equilibrium without specific knowledge of the demand elasticities. As in the case of comparing monopoly equilibrium to competitive equilibrium, we see that the results depend upon the nature of demand. Once again, the explanation lies in the price-quantity trade off. In the case of the capital gains tax, for example, tax payments equal $\theta(p_1 - p_0)L_1$. If the monopolist increases sales in $T = 0$, L_1 decreases but $(p_1 - p_0)$ must increase. This latter effect is not considered by competitors who take prices as given. Whether or not it is profitable for the monopolist to increase sales at $T = 0$ depends on the nature of this trade off. Determinate effects of this tax in the competitive case then become indeterminate in the monopoly situation.

SUMMARY AND CONCLUSIONS

(1) For low levels of demand, a competitive development industry will supply developed land at a price equal to the present value of agricultural returns plus development costs. For higher levels of demand for land in fixed supply, developers will supply land such that the price of developed land appreciates at a rate equal to the developer's discount rate, r, less an amount relating the opportunity costs of land development to current developed land prices. Ricardian rents on land appreciate at rate r and the rate of price appreciation approaches r as the price of developed land becomes high relative to land's yearly return from agriculture. Given the dynamic nature of demand, it is also noted that Ricardian rents on land are generally positive despite the fact that only a small part of total supply may be transacted in any one period.

(2) With land in fixed supply, a monopolist is less likely to develop all his land than a competitive development industry within the same time horizon. If

demand is sufficient for the monopolist to develop all his land profitably, however, he may develop it faster than the competitive industry. The monopolist's problem is to weigh the trade off between a low rate of development and a high rate of price appreciation. In such a situation, the existence of monopoly power is not sufficient for the exercise of monopoly power and, therefore, for resource misallocation. If market power is exercised and all land is developed, then in one period monopoly profits are lower than the associated competitive Ricardian rents.

(3) In the competitive case, a property tax or a capital gains tax will reduce the initial period price of developed land. The property tax will also reduce the second-period price and increase the equilibrium rate of price appreciation. The capital gains tax will lead to a higher rate of development and a higher rate of price appreciation than would prevail in the absence of the tax. The capital gains tax cannot reduce the total amount of land developed over time.

(4) In the situation where demand is sufficient for competitive developers to develop all their land profitably, it does not follow that the incidence of these taxes falls entirely on the developers. The optimal trade off depends on the exact nature of consumer demand. Although their total supply is perfectly inelastic, these taxes lead to an inter-period reallocation of development. The present value of total consumer payments for land will be altered and may decrease, a situation that might be termed a negative tax incidence.

(5) The effect of these taxes on the monopolist's supply is indeterminate. With an *ad valorem* tax on capital gains, for example, the monopolist can reduce the quantity component of total capital gains (equal to price change times quantity) only at the expense of increasing the price change component.

4
The role of uncertainty
and speculation in
the land market

INTRODUCTION

Although we believe the model presented in chapter 3 is very useful for
illuminating some aspects of the land market, its major weakness is that it does
not adequately deal with uncertainty. This is probably not an important short-
coming for a long-run equilibrium situation in which expectations are fairly
stable (such as, for example, most Ontario urban land markets during the
sixties). It is impossible, however, to adequately capture the price movements in
land markets during the seventies without taking explicit account of uncertainty
faced by agents in these markets. The 'long-run' equilibrium model of chapter 3
predicts a smooth, regular price trend in a market with increasing demand (with
Ricardian rents appreciating at some appropriate discount rate), which is inconsistent with the quantum jump in land prices actually observed during the
seventies.

In this chapter we will analyse the effects of uncertainty on the functioning
of the land market. We will focus most of our attention on the case of perfectly
competitive markets, since even with this simplifying assumption, we will see
that uncertainty makes the models extremely complicated. We will however
discuss the conditions necessary for deviation from perfect competition (suitably
defined to incorporate uncertainty). In any competitive market uncertainty
arises from two distinct sources: (1) the uncertainty of future prices; and (2) the
uncertainty of future technology. Since land is a durable good, price uncertainty
will generally lead to *speculation*, i.e., the holding of land for the purposes of
earning a capital gain, so any reasonable model incorporating uncertainty must
include speculation as a possible activity.

The effects of speculation on markets has long been a topic of interest to economists.[1] For well-co-ordinated, competitive markets like the foreign exchange market and the stock market, economic theory argues that speculation serves a useful economic purpose, since speculators bear risk which does not have to be borne by other agents in the market. Theory also argues that speculation will not affect long-run price levels, and speculation will in fact speed the adjustment to long-run equilibrium, and dampen the oscillations of the adjustment.

Although the land market is not as well co-ordinated as the foreign exchange market or the stock market (because, for example, there is no centralized market for land), we will argue that the effects of speculation on long-run equilibrium prices are as theory preducts, if the land market is competitive. However, in the short run, speculation can have a significant effect on prices, and in some cases can cause prices to diverge from their long-run equilibrium levels. This latter conclusion should not be surprising since in recent years the stock market (during the conglomerate boom of the sixties) and the gold market (during recent monetary crises) have provided examples of probable 'speculative bubbles.' Economists seem to think that such occurrences are less likely than evidence suggests, probably because of an attempt to always force their analysis into the usual static, long-run equilibrium framework.

In most industries technological uncertainty, to the extent it is important, is the result of uncertain technological change (occurring e.g. from R and D). Uncertainty about technological change (in the technology of converting raw land into serviced land) has not been an important phenomenon in land markets (although servicing costs have increased). However, technological uncertainty of a different sort does seem to be an important phenomenon in land markets. This uncertainty arises because a developer must not only physically transform raw land into serviced, subdivided land, but he must also gain governmental approval in order to subdivide land. Developers generally always face at least some uncertainty about what a government decision will be in any particular case, and this has seemed to be an increasingly important aspect of land markets in some regions of Ontario during the seventies.

In the next section of this chapter we examine the determinants of 'the' rate of return to 'speculation' in the land market. We abstract from the development process, which is examined in the third section, and focus on the asset demand for land. We would expect that the (random) rate of return on land would bear some relationship to the rates of return on other assets, since common shares, bonds, gold, art, etc. are all assets which are alternatives to land. Some types of

1 The classic references on the role of speculation in competitive markets are Bachelier (1900), and Williams (1935).

land (e.g., the lot of a single family, owner-occupied house) are not exactly like bonds or stocks, since they also provide a flow of non-financial services to the owner, but in this respect land is not different from art, or houses, or some other assets. Therefore, in the next section we develop a model which explains the connection between the rates of return on different types of land and other assets. One of the most important conclusions of this model is that it is incorrect to think in terms of *'the'* rate of return to speculation in land. This is because land is heterogenous with respect to risk. Thus, for example, for some types of land it may be incorrect to infer non-competitive behaviour from an observation of higher than 'normal' rates of return, since in equilibrium, risky land should earn, *on average*, a higher rate of return than less risky assets, in order for holders of such land to be willing to bear the increased risk.

In the third section of this chapter we incorporate uncertainty and specula-tion into a model which is a significantly modified version of the model pre-sented in chapter 3. Spot markets in the consumption composite, raw land, subdivided land, and riskless bonds are included in the model. To be consistent with the institutional framework of the land market, we assume that there are no explicit future markets in these commodities. The model includes both price and technological uncertainty. As we will see, the basic usefulness of the model is derived from the development of a coherent framework for modeling un-certainty and speculation. Although the model is conceptually simple, its analytical complexity makes it difficult to derive many explicit results. It is, however, possible to explain the stylized facts of the short-run dynamics of Ontario land markets during the seventies, using the framework of the model.

LAND AS AN ASSET: 'THE' RATE OF RETURN TO LAND SPECULATION

The model developed in this section is essentially an extension of the Capital Asset Pricing Model (CAPM), which is a model of the determination of values of assets traded on the stock exchange. The main references in the CAPM literature are Sharpe (1964) and Mossin (1966, 1973). We will begin with a model in which we make some very unrealistic assumptions, and then indicate the effects of changing these assumptions.

Consider a model with m investors, $i = 1, ..., m$. The assets available to these investors are n different types of land $j = 1, ..., n$, a non-land risky asset (e.g., some stock portfolio), and a riskless bond. We assume that there is only one non-land risky asset purely for expositional simplicity. The n types of land are not meant to be interpreted as n individual properties, but rather n 'risk classes' of land. For example, in the region of Toronto, vacant land in Scarborough is probably more likely to be developed than land in Ajax, so land in these two regions would be in different risk classes. Differences in zoning or municipalities' attitudes toward development would also generally imply differences in risk class. We assume that all land in a given risk class is homogeneous, so the equilibrium price per unit will be identical for all land transacted in a given risk class.

For simplicity we will restrict ourselves to a one-period model. At the beginning of the period each investor has some (possibly zero) initial stock of different types of land, the 'outside' risky asset, and riskless bonds. We assume that the total stock of different types of land is held by the aggregate of all investors (so we would have to include farmers, for example, as investors in this model). At the beginning of the period investors trade land among themselves and trade the 'outside' risky asset and riskless bonds among themselves and with the 'outside world.' The equilibrium price of different types of land is determined by the model, but the price of the outside risky asset is exogenous.

Initial wealth of the ith investor W_i is

$$W_i = \bar{m}_i + p_s \bar{s}_i + \sum_{j=1}^{m} \bar{z}_{ij} p_j \tag{27}$$

where $\bar{m}_i$ is initial holdings of the riskless asset, $\bar{s}_i$ is initial holdings of the outside risky asset and p_s is its price, and $\bar{z}_{ij}$ is the initial percentage held of land in risk class j with p_j *total equilibrium value* of land of type j.

End of period wealth of the ith investor, Y_i, will be

$$Y_i = rm_i + \tilde{X}s_i + \sum z_{ij} \tilde{X}_j \tag{28}$$

where r is the riskless rate of return, $\tilde{X}$ is the random gross rate of return on the outside risky asset ($\tilde{X} = p_s^{t+1} / p_s^t$), and $\tilde{X}_j$ is the random end of period value of land of type j. Of course an investor's (subjective) probability distribution of the $\tilde{X}_j$'s is based on his expectations about the likelihood of various types of land actually being developed and his estimates of the future value of developed land. The variables m_i, s_i, z_{ij} are equilibrium holdings of the various assets by investor i, which are chosen subject to his budget constraint. For simplicity, let us assume that investor i is in equilibrium initially, so that $\bar{z}_{ij} = z_{ij}$, etc. Then, substituting his budget constraint (27) into (28) we have

$$Y_i = rW_i + (\tilde{X} - rp_s)s_i + \sum_j z_{ij} (\tilde{X}_j - rp_j). \tag{29}$$

We assume that each investor's objective is to maximize his expected utility of end of period wealth, and the ith investor's utility function has the form $U_i =$

$Y_i - c_i Y_i^2$.[2] Initially we will assume that all investors have identical expectations. Later we will relax this assumption. Therefore each investor's choice problem can be written

$$\max_{\{s_i, z_{ij}\}} E\{U_i(Y_i)\}, \tag{30}$$

where Y_i is given by (29), and $U_i = Y_i - c_i Y_i^2$.

The first order conditions for (30) can be written

$$E\{(1 - 2c_i Y_i)(\tilde{X} - rp_s)\} = 0, \tag{31}$$
$$E\{(1 - 2c_i Y_i)(\tilde{X}_j - rp_j)\} = 0, j = 1, ..., n.$$

For purposes of expositional convenience let $X = X_{n+1}, p_s = p_{n+1}, s_i = z_{in+1}$, and let the parameters of the common expectations be $E\{\tilde{X}_j\} = \mu_j$, $\text{cov}(\tilde{X}_j, \tilde{X}_k) = \sigma_{jk}$. Then, taking expectations in (31) and simplifying, the first order conditions for each investor can be written

$$\sum_{k=1}^{n+1} z_{ik}[\sigma_{jk} + (\mu_j - rp_j)(\mu_k - rp_k)] = (\mu_j - rp_j)(1/2c_i - rW_i), \tag{32}$$

where $j = 1, ..., n + 1, i = 1, ..., m$. The final equilibrium conditions for the model require that all land be held,

$$\sum_i z_{ik} = 1, k = 1, ..., n. \tag{33}$$

Equations (32) and (33) determine the z_{ij}'s and the p_j's $(j = 1, ..., n)$. Following the usual analysis in the CAPM literature, it can be shown that

$$z_{ij} = (1/2c_i - rW_i) / \sum_i (1/2c_i - rW_i), j = 1, ..., n, \tag{34}$$

so we get the usual CAPM result that each investor holds a given percentage of *each* type of land. This result is somewhat surprising perhaps, since our model has an extra outside risky asset, and z_{in+1} will generally be different from z_{ij}, $j = 1, ..., n$. Notice that the amount of land any investor i holds will be a decreasing function of c_i, i.e., the more risk averse the investor, the less land he will hold.

---

2 This assumption is not necessary. Any mean-variance utility function will yield the same basic results. See Mossin (1973).

To solve for the equilibrium p_j's, we must make some assumption about the aggregate wealth of the investors. For simplicity let us assume that aggregate *net* holdings of the outside assets is zero, i.e., $\Sigma \bar{m}_i + \bar{z}_{n+1} p_{n+1} = 0$. Also for simplicity, let us assume that $\sigma_{j,n+1} = 0, j = 1, ..., n$ (i.e., the rate of return on the outside asset is not correlated with the rates of return of different types of land). This assumption does not affect the qualitative properties of the solution. With these two assumptions we can solve for the p_j's giving us

$$ p_j = (1/r)\{\mu_j - \sum_{k=1}^{n} \sigma_{jk} / (\Sigma 1/2c_i - \Sigma\mu_k)[1 - (\mu_{n+1} - rp_{n+1})^2 / [\sigma_{n+1}{}^2 + (\mu_{n+1} - rp_{n+1})^2]]\}. \tag{35} $$

The term μ_j/r is the expected discounted value of land of type j, so that the remaining complicated term in (35) can be interpreted as the equilibrium total risk premium required for investors to hold land of type j.

Although some of the assumptions we have made are very unrealistic, (35) is interesting because it illustrates, for this very simple model, how the equilibrium price of land in different risk classes is related to the covariation between returns on land in different risk classes and to the mean, variance, and price of the outside risky asset. Thus, for example, we see from (35) that a decrease in the expected rate of return of the outside risky asset (μ_{n+1}/p_{n+1}) will increase P_j (assuming $\Sigma \sigma_{jk} > 0$).

Examination of (35) makes it clear that 'the' rate of return to land speculation will generally be different for different types of land. Consider, for example, two types of land, j and j' for which $\mu_j = \mu_{j'}$, but $\Sigma \sigma_{jk} > \Sigma \sigma_{j'k}$. Thus land of type j has the same future expected value as land of type j', but it is riskier.[3] We see from (35) that the expected rate of return on land of type $j, (\mu_j / p_j)$, will be greater than the expected rate of return on land of type j'. This is necessary in order for holders of land of type j to be willing to bear the increased riskiness. If expectations are a good predictor of the future (which would be true in a long-run equilibrium), then, on average the realized rate of return on land of type j would be higher than the realized rate of return on land of type j'.

With this very simple model we can analyse the impact on the land market of two important "shocks" experienced by capital markets in Canada during the seventies. The first of these was the enactment of a federal capital gains tax which exempted owner-occupied residences. This tax caused an increase in the investment demand for owner-occupied residences which increased house and land prices. The effect of the tax is somewhat difficult to analyse within the

3 Notice that the appropriate definition of risk is $\Sigma \sigma_{jk}$, not σ_{jj}.

framework of our model, since the tax would change p_{n+1}, which is exogenous to our model. However, we can see that if, as is likely, the effect of the tax was to reduce the (after-tax) expected return on financial assets, our model predicts that land prices will increase. The second shock affecting Canada's capital markets of the seventies was the increasing rate of inflation. Inflation reduced expected *real* returns on financial assets, and our model would again predict that this would raise land prices. We will return to a more detailed analysis of the impact of these two features of the seventies in the next section.

Let us now discuss the appropriateness of our assumptions and possible modifications. Probably the most unrealistic assumption we have made is that investors have identical expectations. It is argued in the CAPM literature that this is perhaps a reasonable approximation to reality for shares trading on the New York Stock Exchange. The basis of this argument is that the stock market is a very well-coordinated, perfectly competitive market, with centralized trading and very efficient information flows. The centralization of the market and SEC regulations regarding provision of information by companies and restrictions on insider trading, etc., insures that a great deal of information is available to investors. The amount and availability of information is also significantly increased by the brokerage houses, which actively engage in gathering, processing, and disseminating information.

The most important difference between the land market and the stock market is the absence of a well co-ordinated centralized land market. Therefore even relatively simple information such as current prices and recent price movements which is freely available in the stock market requires effort to obtain in the land market, and the information is much less reliable. However, the importance of realtors in generating, processing and disseminating information should not be underestimated. Like brokerage houses, the main business of realtors is to earn commissions on sales, and one important service a realtor can provide his client is the provision of information. Of course not all land transactions involve realtors, but a high enough proportion do to make the information disseminating role of realtors an important aspect of the market. In our opinion, the land market is not as informationally inefficient as it is sometimes characterized.

Nevertheless, the assumption of homogeneous expectations is unrealistic. It can be shown (Mossin, 1973) that if investors have heterogenous expectations, the prices determined in the CAPM will be determined by a weighted average of individual expectations, with the weight of each individual depending on his relative size in the given market. Thus the same sort of qualitative properties of the relationship between land prices and covariance of returns on different types of land and the return and variability of non-land assets derived in (35) will still hold.

Because of the relative 'thinness'[4] of the land market in comparison with more well developed asset markets, it is important to understand what we mean by 'relative size' in the preceding paragraph. An agent is small relative to the market if his land holdings are small relative to the total amount of land. Because of the thinness of the market, any agent may represent a significant proportion of land purchases or sales during some period. However, this does not imply that he has significant market power, unless he owns a significant proportion of the potential supply, i.e., unless he owns a significant proportion of the total amount of land. For example, in the stock market, for a thinner stock a large investor might in any one day's trading account for a significant proportion of the total trading in that stock. However, if he does not own a significant proportion of the tradeable stock outstanding, he will not have a significant effect on that month's average price. Of course the stock market is a much more efficient market than the land market, because of well co-ordinated centralized trading and the existence of 'specialists' whose job it is to minimize short-run fluctuations. The absence of a centralized market and specialists in the land market means that individual large trades will have greater impact on short-run average prices. Nevertheless, if all agents are small relative to the market, no agent will have significant market power, i.e., influence over longer-run average prices.

The most important source of the heterogeneity of expectations is that some agents in the land market have better information than others. There seems to be a popular misconception about the effects of this heterogeneity. It is sometimes argued that if an agent has better information, then he has market power, i.e., he can control prices for his own benefit. This is not true. An agent will have market power only if the size of his holdings is large relative to the market. If an agent has better-than-average information, on average he will earn better-than-average returns on his land portfolio, but this is not an indication of market power. We would expect that successful developers and speculators would have better than average information, and therefore that they will earn better than average returns. This is not evidence of market power. Existence of potential market power can be established only by the existence of concentrated ownership.

UNCERTAINTY, SPECULATION, AND THE DEVELOPMENT PROCESS

Our analysis in the preceding section concentrated exclusively on land as an asset. In this section we will analyse how uncertainty and speculation affect the

4 By 'thinness' we mean that there are generally a relatively small number of transactions in the land market, as compared, for example, with the stock market.

development process. We will consider a model which is a suitably modified version of the competitive model developed in chapter 3. In that model we assumed perfect foresight, and argued that that assumption was fairly reasonable for a land market in (dynamic) long-run equilibrium. However, to analyse the short-run dynamics of the land market when not in long-run equilibrium, the assumption of perfect foresight must be dispensed with. In chapter 3 we also ignored the development process, i.e., the process by which raw land is purchased and converted into developed land. Since one of the important sources of uncertainty in the development process arises from the uncertainty about government approval of subdivision plans, we must treat the development process more explicitly in this chapter.

We will divide the agents in the land market into two groups, developers, and non-developers. Developers are agents who have the production capability[5] to convert undeveloped land into developed land. Non-developers are any agents in the land market who do not engage in this production activity, i.e., consumers, farmers, and speculators. Our model will also allow developers to engage in speculative transactions (i.e., buying and selling land without developing it). The agricultural demand for undeveloped land is fairly easy to specify, so we will concentrate on the consumption and speculative demand for land by consumers and speculators. Since consumers are land consumers and potential land speculators, it seems reasonable to aggregate consumers and speculators (not including developers) into one sector, which we will call the consumer sector, and from now on we will call consumers and non-developer speculators, consumers.

Consumers, as in chapter 3, consume the composite consumption good and the services of developed land. They hold their wealth in three possible assets: a riskless asset, undeveloped land, or developed land.[6] For simplicity we assume they consume the services of all developed land which they own, but derive no consumption benefits from their holding of raw land. There are spot markets in the consumption composite, undeveloped and developed land, and the riskless asset. The current and future price of the consumption composite is assumed to be unity, but the future price of undeveloped and developed land is uncertain. In the current period the consumer must decide how much of the consumption composite to consume, and how much undeveloped and developed land to purchase or sell.

A formal model of the consumer's decision making is developed in appendix F. Let L^c be the *total* demand for developed land (which is to be interpreted as

5 An important part of the production capability is the expertise necessary to obtain a subdivision approval.
6 For simplicity, we do not include a non-land risky asset. A non-land risky asset is included in our model in the second section of this chapter.

the demand for land associated with the demand for housing) and λ^c be the *total* demand for undeveloped land (by non-developers). Then our analysis of consumer choice in appendix F leads us to specify market demand functions:

$$L^c = L^c(P, R, I; \underline{E}^c_L), \tag{36}$$

$$\lambda^c = \lambda^c(P, R, I; \underline{E}^c_\lambda),$$

where P is the spot price of developed land, R is the spot price of undeveloped land, and I is the vector of current incomes. The terms $\underline{E}^c_L$ and $\underline{E}^c_\lambda$ are proxies to remind us that the current demand for developed and undeveloped land depends on expectations about future prices and income. We show in the appendix that the properties of an individual consumer's demand functions depend crucially on his expectations about the future. Although these expectations can be considered fixed at a given moment of time, they will generally be influenced by current and past developments in the land market and in other markets. Thus, as we will see, the short-run dynamics of the model resulting from a shock to a previous equilibrium situation will depend crucially on the expectations-forming mechanism of the consumer section.

Now let us consider the developer sector. As we mentioned earlier, it is important to consider the development process explicitly in order to analyse suitably the effects of uncertainty on the land prices and the rate of development. For simplicity, we assume that there are three types of land; undeveloped land, approved land, and developed land. Undeveloped land and developed land have the same interpretation as in the consumer section. Approved land is land which is approved (by the government) for development, but has not yet been fully developed. Developed land is then approved land which is ready to be built on.

Our simple model of the development process works in the following way. Developers buy undeveloped land from farmers, consumers, speculators, and other developers. (We also will allow them to sell undeveloped land, i.e., to speculate.) They then devote resources in order to get their stock of undeveloped land approved for development. We assume that the approval process is uncertain, so that out of a given stock of undeveloped land and expenditure, the amount of land that will actually be approved is uncertain. Land which is approved is then held until a decision is made to develop it. For simplicity we assume that approved land is not traded (this would seem to be consistent with the actual workings of the land market), and approved land is only developed if it is sold in the current period. Therefore, at the beginning of each period the developer has a stock of undeveloped and approved land. He must then decide how much undeveloped land to buy or sell, how much resources should be devoted to the approval process, and how much approved land to develop. At the time of these decisions he knows the current prices of undeveloped and serviced land, but is uncertain about future prices and the amount of land which will be approved.

There is some difficulty involved in building a simple model of a developer, since there is no agreement in the economics literature on what an intertemporal firm's objective should be in an environment of uncertainty. For simplicity we will assume that the firm's objective is to maximize expected discounted profits.[7] Therefore the firm's objective is

$$\max E_0 \left\{ \sum_0^\infty (1+\delta)^{-\tau} \Pi_t \right\},$$ (37)

where Π_t is profits at time t, δ is the firm's discount rate, and E_0 is the expected value conditional on the values of the random variables at time o. The discount rate, or 'required rate of return,' δ, will reflect the inherent riskiness faced by the firm, so that if, for example, for some reason the development business became riskier, we would expect that δ would increase.

Let $\bar{L}_t$ be the stock of land held at the beginning of period t, which has been approved for subdivision. Let L_t be the amount of land serviced (and sold) during period t. Finally, let $\bar{\lambda}_t$ be the stock of undeveloped land held at the beginning of period t, and λ_t the amount of undeveloped land purchased during period t. Then

$$\bar{L}_t = \bar{L}_{t-1} - L_{t-1} + f(\bar{\lambda}_{t-1} + \lambda_{t-1}; X)$$ (38)

is the equation determining the stock of approved land held at the beginning of time t. The expression $f(\bar{\lambda}_{t-1} + \lambda_{t-1}; X)$ represents the amount of undeveloped land newly approved for subdivision during period $(t-1)$, where X is the amount of expenditure involved in the approval process, so that $f(\bar{\lambda}_{t-1} + \lambda_{t-1}; X) \leq \bar{\lambda}_{t-1} + \lambda_{t-1}$ and $f_X \geq 0$. The actual amount of undeveloped land approved for subdivision from a given stock of undeveloped land and expenditure is uncertain, due to the uncertainties involved in the government approval process. Therefore $f(\ )$ is a random variable.

The equation giving the stock of undeveloped land available at time t can now be written

---

7 A justification of this assumption can be found in Arrow (1964), and Scheffman (1976).

$$\bar{\lambda}_t = \bar{\lambda}_{t-1} + \lambda_{t-1} - f(\bar{\lambda}_{t-1} + \lambda_{t-1}; X). \tag{39}$$

Now the equation determining profits at time t can be derived,

$$\Pi_t = (P_t - s)L_t - R_t \lambda_t + q(\bar{L}_t + \bar{\lambda}_t + \lambda_t - L_t) - X, \tag{40}$$

where s is the per unit costs of lot servicing, etc. (not including X), and q is the agricultural return on land.

For simplicity, let us consider a two-period model. (It is shown in appendix F that the solution of (37) can always be described as a solution of a sequence of two-period problems.) The developer's maximization problem then can be written

$$\max_{\{L_o, \lambda_o, X\}} E\left\{(P_o - s)L_o - R_o \lambda_o + q(\bar{L} + \bar{\lambda} + \lambda_o - L_o) - X \right.$$
$$+ (1 + \delta)^{-1} [(P_1 - s)[\bar{L} - L_o + f(\bar{\lambda} + \lambda_o; X)]$$
$$\left. + R_1 [\bar{\lambda} + \lambda_o - f(\bar{\lambda} + \lambda_o; X)]]\right\}, \tag{41}$$

where $\bar{L}, \bar{\lambda}$ are the stocks held at the beginning of period o. The random variables in (41) are P_1, R_1, and $f(\ )$. Given our assumption that approved land is not developed unless it is sold in the current period, the variable P_1 is to be interpreted as next period's price, if next period's price is greater than $R_1 + s$, otherwise it is $R_1 + s$, Similarly, $R_1 \geq v$, so that $P_1 - s \geq v$ (v is the agricultural value of land).

The first order conditions for (41) are

(i) $(P_o - s - q) - (1 + \delta)^{-1} E\{P_1 - s\} \geq 0$ if $0 < L_o \leq \bar{L}$,

$\qquad \leq 0$ if $L_o = 0$,

(ii) $- R_o + q + (1 + \delta)^{-1} E\{(P_1 - S)f_1 + R_1(1 - f_1)\} \leq 0, \lambda_o \geq -\bar{\lambda}$

(iii) $- 1 + (1 + \delta)^{-1} E\{(P_1 - s)f_2 - R_1 f_2\} \leq 0, E \geq 0.$ \hfill (42)

Although the three expressions in (42) are somewhat complicated, they have a straightforward interpretation. For example, if all expressions hold with equality, (42) requires that the expected rate of return on the marginal dollar invested in undeveloped land, developed land, or in the approval process, be δ. If (42 (i)) holds with equality it can be written:

$$(P_o - s - q - v(1 + \delta)^{-1}) - (1 + \delta)^{-1} E\{P_1 - s - v\} = 0. \tag{43}$$

The interpretation of (43) is clear, in light of our analysis in chapter 3. In order for the developer to both develop some land and carry part of his stock of approved land into the future, expected Ricardian rents must appreciate at rate δ. In 'normal' circumstances (i.e., when prices are such that the developer develops some but not all of his current stock of approved land, (42 (i)) will hold with equality. In that case, if developers have identical expectations and risk aversion (δ), then P_0 will be determined by (42 (i)), if $E\{P_1\}$ is not a function of R_0. From (43) we also have

$$E\{P_1\} / P_0 = (1 + \delta)[1 - (q + s - s(1 + \delta)^{-1}) / p_0], \tag{44}$$

so that if (42 (i)) holds with equality, equilibrium prices must be such that the expected rate of price appreciation is less than δ.

Since L and λ are measured in the same units, it is reasonable to assume that $f_1 \leqq 1$. Recalling that $P_1 - s \geqq R_1 \geqq v$ by definition, if (42 (ii)) holds with equality and $L_0 > 0$, from (42 (i)) and (42 (ii)) we have

$$R_0 - q - v(1 + \delta)^{-1} \leqq (1 + \delta)^{-1} E\{P_1 - s - v\}$$
$$\leqq P_0 - s - v(1 + \delta)^{-1}, \tag{45}$$

so that the Ricardian rent earned on undeveloped land will be less than that earned on developed land (if the probability of $f_1 < 1$ is positive).

For simplicity let us assume that P_1 and f, and R_1 and f are (statistically) independent. Then (42 (ii)) can be written

$$E\{R_1\} / R_0 \leqq (1 + \delta)[1 - (q + E\{P_1 - s - R_1\}E f_1) / R_0], \tag{46}$$

and (42 (iii)) can be written

$$(1 + \delta) \geqq E\{P_1 - s - R_1\} E\{f_2\}. \tag{47}$$

From (46) it is easily seen that equilibrium prices must be such that the expected rate of price appreciation of undeveloped land is also less than δ. We can also write (42 (ii)) as:

$$[R_0 - q - v(1 + \delta)^{-1}] - (1 + \delta)^{-1}[E\{R_1\} - v]$$
$$\geqq (1 + \delta)^{-1} E\{P_1 - s - R_1\} E\{f_1\}, \tag{48}$$

so that *expected* Ricardian rents on undeveloped land (measured as the deviation between the price of undeveloped land and agricultural value) will appreciate at a rate less than δ (assuming $E\{P_1\} > E\{R_1 + s\}$).

Assuming (42 (i-iii)) hold with equality, P_o, λ_o, and X are determined by (42), given R_o. Therefore $\partial P_o / \partial R_o$, $\partial \lambda_o / \partial R_o$, and $\partial X / \partial R_o$ can be determined in the usual way. However, the signs of these derivatives will depend on how expectations are formed, i.e., on the relationship between $E\{P_1\}$, $E\{R_1\}$ and R_o. (The details are worked out in appendix F.) However, assuming reasonable properties of $E\{P_1\}$ and $E\{R_1\}$, some general conclusions can be made. For example, if $E\{P_1\}$ increases (from, for example, new industrial development leading to an expected increase in future employment in the urban area), and if (42 (i)) holds with equality before and after the change, then P_o will increase. The mechanism operating here is that at the original P_o, developers slow down development at the original P_o because of the new $E\{P_1\}$, which has the effect of raising P_o. It is very important to understand that this is *not* the result of market power being exercised by developers. Rather, it is due to a shift of the *competitive* supply function because of revised expectations. Similarly, an increase in $E\{P_1\}$ would tend to increase developers' demand for undeveloped land at every R_o. If developers expected a more restrictive approval process, so that $E\{f_1\}$ falls for every $\bar{\lambda} + \lambda_o$, developers' demand for undeveloped land would decrease at every R_o, which would generally slow down the future rate of development and increase future prices. Thus we see that expectations are very important in determining price in the short run, and of course in determining the short-run dynamics of the model.

In our model the effects of changes in uncertainty operate through presumed changes in the risk adjusted discount rate δ. Thus, for example, if the development business becomes riskier (from, for example, increased uncertainty about the approval process) we would expect that δ would increase. If the expected values of P_1, R_1 and f are not changed by this increase in riskiness, the effects can be determined easily by considering the effects of an increase in δ on (42). If (42 (i)) holds with equality before and after the increase in riskiness, P_o will be reduced. Similarly, if (42 (ii)) holds with equality, the demand for λ_o will fall at each R_o. Again, these effects have nothing to do with market power, they are merely the result of shifts in *competitive* supply and demand functions as a result of changing expectations.

Now let us consider the equilibria in the markets for undeveloped and developed land. Initially let us assume that $E\{P_1\}$ and $E\{R_1\}$ are not functions of R_o and P_o. Suppose the equilibrium is such that (42 (i), (ii), and (iii)) hold with equality. Let $\bar{P}_o$ be the solution of (42 (i)). Then the equations determining market equilibrium are

(i) $L^c(\bar{P}_0, R_0, I; \underline{E}^c_L) - \bar{L}^c - L_0 = 0, 0 < L_0 < \bar{L}^D$

(ii) $\lambda^c(\bar{P}_0, R_0, I; \underline{E}^c_\lambda) + \lambda^D(\bar{P}_0, R_0) - \bar{\lambda}^c - \bar{\lambda}^o = 0,$ \hfill (49)

where $\bar{L}^c$ and $\bar{\lambda}^c$ are the initial stocks of developed and undeveloped land held by consumers, $\bar{\lambda}^c$ is the initial stock of undeveloped land held by developers, $\bar{L}^D$ is the total potential production of developed land by developers (i.e., the current stock of approved land), and $\lambda^D(\bar{P}_0, R_0)$ is the total demand for undeveloped land by developers.

In this simple model R_0 is determined by (49 (ii)), and then (49 (i)) determines L_0. Therefore in the short run, the price of developed land is determined by (42 (i)) (assuming equality), which under our assumptions is independent of the market for undeveloped land. However the actual rate of development is *not* independent of the market for undeveloped land. Shocks affecting the market for undeveloped land will have a greater effect on the rate of development the more elastic is L^c with respect to R_0. We would expect the 'consumption' demand for developed land to be inelastic with respect to R_0, while the 'speculative' demand for developed land would be relatively more elastic with respect to R_0. Therefore shocks affecting the market for undeveloped land will have a greater effect on the rate of development, the greater is the 'speculative' demand for developed land. Shocks affecting the market for developed land will generally have a significant effect on the price of undeveloped land since changes in P_0 will be likely to change expectations about the future value of undeveloped land. For example, a shock which unexpectedly increased P_0 would be likely to increase $E\{P_1\}$, and so increase R_0.

A combination of increasing demand and a reduction in approvals can result in the amount of development being constrained by the stock of approved land. In that case (42 (i)) will no longer hold with equality with the result that P_0 is no longer determined by (42 (i)). In this case P_0 is now a variable in (49) but $L_0 = \bar{L}^D$, which means that the price of developed land is no longer insulated from shocks in the market for undeveloped land. However the rate of development is now determined exogenously by the stock of approved land.

THE ONTARIO LAND SPECULATION TAX

We will now consider the effects of a tax such as the Ontario Land Speculation Tax.[8] This tax is levied on capital gains earned on land which has not been suitably 'improved' by the seller. In its amended form the tax will not affect

8 The tax is explained in detail in chapter 7.

developers in their development activities, since there will be no tax on land which the developer actually develops. The tax is also not levied on owner-occupied land. For expectations constant, the effect of the tax will be to reduce consumer-speculator's demand for undeveloped land, and to a significantly lesser degree reduce the developers' demand for undeveloped land (reflecting a lower expected return on potential speculation). The effect of the tax on the demand for developed land is ambiguous. The lower expected return on non-owner occupied developed land would reduce this component of the total demand for developed land. However, since the tax is not levied on owner occupied land, this type of land is now a more favourable investment relative to undeveloped land and non-owner occupied land. Therefore the net effect may be to either increase or decrease the demand for developed land. The net effect is probably more likely to be a decrease in demand the larger is the current demand for non-owner occupied land.

Let us assume first that equilibrium is characterized by (42 (i)) holding with equality. Then (assuming no change in developers' expectations) $\bar{P}_0$ will not change in the short run. The fall in demand for undeveloped land will un-ambiguously reduce R_0. In appendix F we show that this will reduce P_0. How-ever, the effect on the amount of development is ambiguous, because of the ambiguity of the effect on the demand for developed land. This is because even at the lower P_0, the demand for developed land may be lower, so that it is quite possible that in the short run the speculation tax would have a small effect on the price of developed land and slow the rate of development.

Suppose now that the tax is levied when the original equilibrium situation is such that the constraint on the stock of approved land is binding, so that (42 (i)) does not hold with equality. In this case P_0 is determined by the demand for developed land. The market for developed land in Toronto was approximately in this situation at the time of the imposition of the tax. In this case the tax cannot have an effect on the amount of development in the short run, since $L_0 = \bar{L}^D$. As before, the tax should reduce R_0. However, the effect on P_0 is ambiguous be-cause of the ambiguity of the effect on the demand for developed land. It is possible that the tax could increase P_0. This would be a result of the increased relative attractiveness of owner-occupied land. Again, this is probably less likely the larger the original demand for non-owner occupied developed land.

Since the tax would tend to reduce consumer-speculator's demand for un-developed land more than developers' demand for undeveloped land, the tax will result in a higher percentage of undeveloped land being held by developers and farmers. This effect is likely to be undesirable for two reasons. First, if there is a problem of potential concentration of ownership by developers of raw land, this problem will be exacerbated. Secondly, the shifting of the holding of undeveloped land more towards developers and farmers changes both the bearing of risk in the market and the land assembly process. Speculators who actually hold undeveloped land must on average be less risk averse than developers, since the probability distribution of the return to their holdings must be less favourable than the probability distribution of returns on developers' holdings of undeveloped land. This is because speculators do not have the production capability to produce developed land. Therefore since the required rate of return for bearing risk is a cost which will be reflected in the price of developed land, a shifting of risk to more risk averse developers will eventually be reflected, in the long run, in a higher price for developed land, and consequently, a slower rate of development. The fact that speculators probably also improve the efficiency of the land assembly process reinforces this conclusion. Therefore, as in chapter 3, we conclude that the speculation tax will impair the efficiency of the land market (if it is competitive) in the long run. However, as we will see, the short-run effects of the tax may be beneficial in some circumstances.

AN EXPLANATION OF THE TORONTO REAL ESTATE BOOM OF THE SEVENTIES

We will now attempt to interpret the stylized facts of the Toronto land market of the early seventies in terms of our simple model. We showed in the second section of this chapter that the prices and rates of return on different types of land would be related to the return on other assets. The two most important 'shocks' affecting the demand for land during the early seventies were the enactment of a federal capital gains tax which exempted owner-occupied residences and the increasing rate of inflation. The capital gains tax probably increased the demand for developed land because it increased the demand for owner-occupied residences. The unanticipated accelerating rate of inflation in the early seventies resulted in a very poor performance by most major financial assets. Foremost among these were common shares. Even less risky instruments such as government bonds were yielding poor real returns because of the unanticipated accelerating rate of inflation. The poor returns on financial assets resulted in a shift in demand towards non-financial assets such as gold, art, and land. The shift in asset demand plus the increase in demand resulting from population growth resulted in a total growth of demand which was probably unanticipated by developers.

At this same time the developers in the Toronto area were experiencing a tightening of the approval process which had begun in the sixties. This tightening was mainly the result of three government actions. First, the provincial government thought that development was proceeding too fast in the sixties and therefore cautioned municipalities to slow their growth. Secondly, the approval process was made more complicated by institution of regional municipalities within the Toronto region. Associated with these regional municipalities were plans that were meant to reduce uncertainty about the future pattern of development by laying out where development could and could not take place in the future. Unfortunately these plans probably had an opposite effect, since major changes which contravened the purposes of the plans were continually made (e.g., as to what land was to be designated green belt) due to political and other considerations. The regional municipalities also made the subdivision approval process more complicated, since they imposed a new hurdle in the approval process without getting rid of any of the previously existing hurdles. Finally, the government had not foreseen the increase in demand, so construction of main sewer trunk lines, etc. was not completed as fast as it should have been.

The combination of the unexpected increased demand and restriction of approvals and serviced land meant that in the early seventies, in terms of our simple model, the approved land capacity had been reached. (This does not mean that all approved land was developed and being built on as in our simple model, since development and building take time.) In terms of the model, once this capacity is reached, the rate of price appreciation (which is bounded above by δ before capacity is reached), can be arbitrarily large. The actual rate will be determined by the excess of demand over capacity. Thus lot prices began to 'take off' in the early seventies, and of course this was reflected in house prices. This then caused a revision in expectations about future prices by both developers and consumer-speculators which had three effects. First, the capital gains realized on used housing encouraged a substitution from other assets and encouraged some consumers to purchase a house earlier than they had originally intended. Secondly, the increase in house and lot prices revised expectations about future house and lot prices which increased the speculative demand for undeveloped land and non-owner occupied houses. Finally, the change in developers' expectations caused an upward shift in the supply of new housing.

Therefore the effect of the 'take off' of lot prices was to increase the demand for developed land, increase the speculative demand for undeveloped land, and possibly reduce the supply (i.e., shift up the supply curve) of developed land. Since the supply of developed land could not significantly increase, this second round increase in demand for developed land caused a further rise in the price of developed land. Normally a boom such as this will be dampened by 'profit taking' on the part of current holders of the asset. However, the major part of the total demand for developed land is a consumption, not a speculative demand. A homeowner may sell his house to realize a capital gain, but he would then generally buy another house, leaving total demand unchanged. Of course there was some 'profit taking' by owners of non-owner occupied housing, but this was not sufficient to prevent total demand from increasing. Consumption demand is not such an important component of the total demand for undeveloped land, but as long as lot prices continued to rise and be extrapolated into expectations about future lot prices this was reflected in the price of undeveloped land.

A speculative bubble such as we have described cannot continue indefinitely, since demand must continually increase to justify past expectations, which requires more and more 'new blood' in the market. It is not clear how long the bubble would have continued to grow without government action, since prices continued to rise strongly until the imposition of the speculation tax. The imposition of the tax had a very beneficial short-run effect in reducing the speculative demand for developed land, and stabilizing prices.

Although we can claim no special expertise with regard to other urban areas in Canada, we believe our analysis does explain the real estate boom experienced in most major urban areas in Canada during the seventies. The underlying factors which increased the asset demand for land were of course common to all Canadian urban areas. The fact that the boom started in Toronto is the result of two factors. The first of these is the relative tightness of the land market in Toronto. We suspect that the length of time before the boom started in other urban areas is closely related to the amount of slack in the land market and housing industry in those areas. The second major factor in the Toronto case was the large influx of foreign real estate investment into the Toronto area.

The bursting of the speculative bubble has not been accompanied by a rapid decline in prices, as we would expect to occur, for example, in the stock market. By late 1976 there was a slight fall in nominal prices of at least some types of houses, and a significant fall in real house prices from their peak. (Of course the slow down in the housing market was partially the result of high mortgage rates.) However the fall was tempered by two factors. The first of these was a shift towards earlier purchase of homes by first time house buyers which was a response to the explosion of house prices. This shift of course was not affected by the Speculation Tax. The second factor was the decision by builders and sellers of old houses to 'hold out.' For example, there was a significant increase in builders' inventories of new houses and especially in the average time from listing to sale for MLS listed houses. It is impossible to determine the current price of speculative undeveloped land (e.g., land in the Barrie area, where a significant proportion of the speculative activity took place), since there have been virtually no transactions in this market since the imposition of the Speculation Tax. Evidently the speculators still in the market when the bubble burst are still holding, except for a few who have defaulted on their mortgages.

It appears now that in the short run lot prices will probably not fall significantly (and could possibly rise somewhat) since there is still a shortage of serviced land. However some major servicing projects are due to be completed in the next few years which will make available a vast new supply of potentially 'developable' land. In our opinion this will cause a significant fall in real lot prices towards their previous levels if the Toronto land market is competitive (which is the conclusion of our empirical study in chapter 5), since current rents on developed land will be inconsistent with competition and the eventual increase in potential supply. Since Toronto continues to grow, the model of chapter 2 suggests that in the long run real lot prices will be somewhat higher than they were in the late sixties.

Forecasts about the rate of fall of real lot prices from their present levels are also clouded by the uncertainty connected with two government actions. One very important factor in determining how fast lot prices will fall is the provincial government's decision on the future form of its rent control program. The current rent control legislation has resulted in a virtual standstill in the production of rental housing. If this should continue the relative demand for owner-occupied housing may significantly increase, which would result in upward pressure on housing and land prices.

Recent statements by the federal government indicate that it is seriously considering making a portion of mortgage interest tax-deductible. If such a proposal is enacted, of course the demand for owner-occupied housing will increase, which would raise housing and land prices. Therefore, if rent control continues and mortgage interest is made tax deductible, it is quite conceivable that another boom in housing and land prices may result.

SUMMARY AND CONCLUSIONS

In this chapter we considered explicitly the effects of uncertainty and speculation on the functioning of the land market. We showed that the rate of return on different types of land (which differ with respect to risk) will be related to each other and to the rates of return and risk of non-land assets. We found that the presence of uncertainty and the existence of agents with better information than others does not imply the existence of market power. Market power will exist only if there is concentration in the ownership of undeveloped land or in the production of serviced lots.

A model of the development process was developed which incorporated both price uncertainty, and uncertainty about the subdivision approval process. Within the context of this model we explained the housing and land market booms of the seventies. It was argued that the long-run effects of speculation are beneficial, since speculators bear risks which would otherwise have to be borne by more risk-averse agents, and that speculators provide a useful economic role in the land assembly process. However, in the short run speculation can cause prices to diverge from their long-run equilibrium levels, and we argued that this was the case in Toronto in the seventies. We argued that the short-run effects of the Ontario Speculation Tax were beneficial, since its imposition stopped the speculative boom. However, the long-run effects of the tax will be undesirable because of the inefficient shifting of risk bearing which it will cause. Finally, we believe that current (real) land prices in the Toronto area are above their long-run equilibrium level. However, if rent control is continued in Ontario and the federal government makes mortgage interest tax deductible, it is conceivable that current land prices are near or even below long-run equilibrium levels. Even if these two policies are not adopted, land prices may remain above the long-run equilibrium level in the short run, however, until the main servicing facilities which are currently under construction are completed.

5

An empirical investigation
of land ownership in
the Toronto region

INTRODUCTION

The theoretical component of this study was designed to arrive at an understanding of the land development process: the timing and spatial character of land development and the character of land price movements over time. That component identified important parameters such as lot servicing costs, agricultural opportunity costs, market power, and attitude of land investors toward risk. Relationships among these variables were then developed to generate a model of the land development process and to analyse the effect of various taxes on the rate of development.

The theoretical results clearly suggest that the effects of government intervention into the land market will depend on such things as the existence of market power. In the case of a capital gains tax such as the Ontario Land Speculation Tax, for example, the results suggest that the tax will increase the rate of land development in early years and increase the equilibrium rate of price appreciation if the land market is competitive. If the land market is not competitive, however, the tax may have exactly the opposite effects. The monopolist can reduce the quantity component of total capital gains (equal to price change times quantity) only at the expense of increasing the price change component. If the latter effect outweighs the former, the capital gains tax will lead the monopolist to develop land slower than he would in the absence of the tax.

These results have identified a number of interesting empirical questions, the answers to which appear to be critical in any attempt to assess the present and

future impact of government policy on land development. Using Metropolitan Toronto as a case study, the first and primary empirical question that we have addressed in this project is whether or not there is sufficient ownership concentration in undeveloped land around Toronto to suggest the existence of significant market power. First, there have been charges laid by a number of researchers that there is significant ownership concentration in Toronto. We have found the research on which these charges are based to be unsatisfactory. Second, as noted above, any policy prescription we can offer to speed development and reduce land prices must depend on whether or not there is ownership concentration.

A few words should be said at this point concerning previous research on the subject of ownership concentration in the Toronto land market. In particular, we should like to comment on the work of Spurr (1974, 1976) which has received a good deal of attention recently. We regard a portion of this as open to misinterpretation, employing a methodology that practically guarantees findings of high concentration no matter what the true market structure happens to be. Spurr (1976) presents statistics on page 112, for example, that were derived from his Development Corporations Survey. Spurr seems to give the impression that the total amount of land reported in this survey forms the appropriate universe of land to be used for compiling ownership concentration figures. Such a methodology would give, for example, the amount of land held by the top four developers as a percentage land held by the top forty developers. Not surprisingly, this would show that concentration of ownership is 'high' (the top 4 own 58.65 per cent of the total and the top 6 own 76.74 per cent).

The most important reason why this methodology produces meaningless results is that it grossly underestimates the true amount of undeveloped land that is available for future development. Our research demonstrates that there are literally hundreds of agents currently holding land in the Toronto area. Many of these agents are private individuals who hold enough land to rank in the top 25 land holders. Such individuals were not, of course, picked up in the survey. Further, well over one hundred small development and speculative holding companies that were not in the survey hold acreage well in excess of Toronto's development needs for the next ten years. The result of Spurr's methodology is that the proper universe of undeveloped land for estimating ownership concentration is somewhere in the neighbourhood of three times larger than the figure he compiles.

Another piece of questionable research on the Toronto area was done by Dennis and Fish (1972). They argue that there is significant concentration of land ownership in Toronto on the basis of the fact that the top six developers in

Toronto control enough land to satisfy the estimated land requirement for ten years. This conclusion is absurd, suffering from the same inability to perceive the relevant universe of land that Spurr's work suffers from. We must emphasize that the relevant questions are what percentage of the total universe do the top developers hold and what percentage of actual development do the top developers account for. The former question is addressed in this chapter and the latter is addressed in a companion study by Muller (1976). Muller's study shows that the 10 largest subdividers accounted for 59 per cent of dwelling unit approvals during the period 1971-3 and that concentration falls off rapidly thereafter, the top 24 accounting for 75.5 per cent. It is most unfortunate that this work by Dennis and Fish seems to be influencing public policy and political debate (see, for example, Lewis (1972). Public policy based on erroneous notions can have potentially disastrous effects.

In any case, the lack of ownership data and the improper methodology used in compiling what data do exist led us to undertake a direct sample of land ownership. The methodology used to construct this sample and the resulting sample itself is described in the following section. Subsequent sections present the results of the sample and discuss the results in the spirit of the traditional industrial organization literature. These sections, then, analyse the issue of the possible existence of market power on the basis of concentration ratios, barriers to entry, and the barriers to effective collusion.

SAMPLE DESIGN[1]

Any attempt to analyse market concentration must immediately confront the issue of defining the market. In the case of Toronto, the amount of undeveloped land in the hinterland depends, of course, on how far one is willing to travel from the Metro core. It was precisely this issue that led us to develop the analysis of ownership concentration and market power in chapter 2. That analysis argues that with land spatially differentiated by transport costs, 'significant' concentration of ownership within subsets of land at a fixed commuting distance from the urban core is sufficient for the existence of market power if the amount of land held by large landowners is 'significant' relative to an appropriately defined universe of undeveloped and developed residential land.

On the basis of the theory developed in chapter 2, we decided to examine ownership of undeveloped land within a 30- to 45-minute commuting distance

1 A good deal of the information used in forming this sample was derived from developers, municipal and regional planners, realtors, and government officials interested in the land market. The authors gratefully acknowledge this assistance without which a study of this type would not have been possible.

to major metro employment centres.[2] The 30-minute figure is approximately the current boundary of completely built-up areas. Since the ownership of undeveloped land is likely to be more concentrated than the ownership of undeveloped plus developed residential land (which chapter 2 argues is the correct universe for judging concentration), the decision to sample only undeveloped land should result in an upward bias of the concentration figures. A second requirement was that land included in the sample be serviceable with all required utilities within 5 years. Lack of planned trunk sewers in such areas as Vaughan eliminated significant areas of land on this basis. We were somewhat skeptical, however, to eliminate land from the sample on the basis of current zoning restrictions. Our interviews with planners and developers led us to have little faith in the permanence of these restrictions.

The universe of land around Metro that satisfied these restrictions on commuting distance and servicing is quite large. That universe is also characterized by a number of ambiguities, especially in connection with sewer servicing. The new York-Pickering servicing scheme, for example, will theoretically permit sewer servicing for large areas of Vaughan, Richmond Hill, and Markham within a certain drainage basin. Yet the capacity of the planned trunk sewer is not large enough to permit housing construction over the entire drainage basin. In this situation, we determined from planners what areas of the drainage basin were unlikely to be allocated any trunk sewer capacity and left this land out of the universe under consideration.[3]

A second major problem of definition was connected with the land held by the government in the North Pickering project area. It is uncertain at this point what the government will eventually do with this land, especially with the suspension of the planned Pickering airport. Our decision was not to treat this land

2 The areas falling within these limits were inferred from a number of studies, but especially from the studies done for the Metropolitan Toronto Transportation Plan Review as noted in the references at the end of this study. Since we are dealing with questions about what will be the case in the future, there are, of course, uncertainties about precisely what land should be included in this commuting land.

3 There are a number of subdivision plans currently submitted for approval in the land areas judged not likely to be developed due to lack of servicing capacity. Nothing prevents a developer from submitting a plan that is contradictory to municipal or regional plans, local zoning, or provincial green belts, etc. Further, some such plans could be approved for subdivision and allocated servicing due in no small part to political corruption. Planners seem to be keenly aware of this fact and seem quick to take it into consideration when indicating what areas in which subdivision plans have been submitted will or will not be successfully developed. If there is a sample bias here, it is clearly toward over-representing the large developers in the sample.

as part of the universe of 'developable' land. This decision gives a definite down-ward bias to the universe of land under consideration if the government decides to release significant quantities of this land (over 20,000 acres) for development. Whether or not a decision to release this land will raise or lower the concentra-tion figures, however, will depend on the method by which the government disposes of the land. If the land were to be sold off to the large developers, concentration could increase. If the land was sold to small developers, or if the government itself decided to enter the development business, concentration would decrease.

Having defined an appropriate universe, we drew a sample of 71,600 acres that satisfied our restrictions on commuting distance and servicing. Sampling choices were made by picking concession lots of 200 acres each from the areas that planners identified as satisfying our restrictions. No area that planners thought satisfied our sampling criterion was left out. It must be emphasized, however, that because of uncertainty, our sample is not a 100 per cent sample of the land (in this commuting range) that may be developed in the next ten years. The universe was chosen partly on the basis of town and regional planners' best guesses as to what land will be allocated servicing capacity. The planners we interviewed were the first to admit that this is an uncertain exercise. It will certainly be the case that some land that was excluded from our sample on the grounds that it would not get trunk sewer servicing in the next five years (e.g., some land in southern Vaughan) will get such servicing and be developed while some land included in the sample will not be developed before the currently planned capacity is used up. However, our sample included all large holdings of residential land of large developers within the sample area, so that if anything, our sample is biased towards indicating the presence of concentration.

Ownership data for the sample area were compiled from the assessment rolls of Brampton, Markham, Mississauga, Pickering, Richmond Hill, and Vaughan, the six towns in the sample space. It should be pointed out that there are two possible sources of error in using assessment roll data instead of registry records. First, the legal owners (individuals or firms) are under no legal requirement to register under their own names in the assessment rolls. There is no conceivable incentive to lie, however, since the legal owner always appears in the registry rolls.[4] It is also true that in all situations in which we did know the legal owner

---

4 Firms are permitted to do business under names other than their incorporated name pro-vided that the other names are listed on their incorporation papers. These other names are referred to as style names. All style names of companies (or the companies of all style names as the case may be) were compiled in connection with the corporate search done for the effective ownership sample. Nominal ownership statistics given below in-cluded all acreage listed under the style names of each company.

(particularly, in the case of large holdings by large developers) there was no discrepancy between the true owner and the name appearing on the assessment roll. A second source of error is that there may be some lag between the sale of a land parcel and the appearance of the new owner's name on the assessment rolls. The advantage of using the assessment rolls instead of the registry rolls lies in the fact that sampling costs using assessment rolls are only a fraction of the costs using registry rolls. Most of this saving is in terms of time given the different formats of the two types of records, but substantial savings are also realized by avoiding the various charges assessed for examining registry records. We estimate that for our given expenditures on data collection, the use of assessment rolls allowed us to sample two to four times as many acres than we could have sampled using registry records. In our estimation, the possible errors introduced by this method were far outweighed by the gain in information obtained from a larger sample.

Specific sample locations are listed in Table 1 under the heading 'full sample.'[5] All concession lots are 200 acres, though the boundary between Richmond Hill and Markham splits concession 3E giving each town 100 acres in the relevant lots.

One issue that we had to confront was that our sample area included far more land than will be developed in the next fifteen years. Further, all land in the sample does not have equal probability of being developed over that time horizon or especially over a shorter one of say five or ten years. Some owners in the area have assembled land parcels large enough for efficient subdivision while others have not. Some land is properly zoned for residential development while other land is not. Similarly, some landowners have begun the long process of seeking subdivision approval while other owners have not. This latter type of land is on stream in the sense that there is a good probability that the owner can develop the land should he choose to do so. Land that is at present unzoned, incompatible with official plans, and without a subdivision request at present being processed, on the other hand, has virtually no chance of being developed in the next five years and little chance of being developed within the next ten years. The subdivision approval process alone, on properly zoned land, has been taking three years. The point here is that the relevant universe of land available for development depends upon a choice of time horizon in addition to depending upon the servicing factors mentioned above. The red tape of the subdivision

5 A map of the sample area is shown in Figure 5, with specific sample locations shown by the hatch lines. For the reader not familiar with Toronto, the area shown is bounded to the south by Lake Ontario, with the core area of Toronto located near the shore line in the middle of the region marked Metropolitan Toronto. The main transit corridors to other metropolitan areas run east-west through the region from Pickering to Mississauga.

Figure 5
Ownership sample space

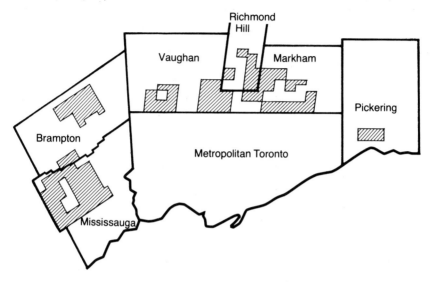

approval process is substantial, involving three levels of government (municipal, regional, and provincial) and literally hundreds of official steps. (We are not asserting that this process is unproductive, only that it probably could be carried out more quickly.)

We took this problem into account by forming a second sample which was simply a sub-sample of the full sample. On the basis of our interviews with planners and studies of official plans, we were able to determine what land included in the sample was unlikely to be developed in the next ten years owing to the reasons just developed. This land was then eliminated from the sample leaving the second sample which we shall refer to as the 'restricted sample.' As with the full sample, our restricted sample is, if anything, biased towards exhibiting concentration, since all large holdings of large developers were included in the restricted sample. The sample locations for this acreage are shown in the right-hand side of Table 1.

One point remains to be made in connection with sample design. In collecting the data, all holdings under two acres were immediately eliminated unless one firm or individual held several such parcels. Such parcels are unlikely to account for significant housing starts in the next ten years and their elimination cut data collection costs drastically. Subdivision approvals will not be applied for or granted for areas anywhere near that small size, and developers have indicated to

TABLE 1

Sample domains – gross acreage

City or Town	Full Sample			Restricted sample		
	Conces sion	Lots	Acres	Conces- sion	Lots	Acres
Brampton	1E	11-15	1000	1E	11-15	1000
	2E	11-15	1000	2E	11-15	1000
	3E	6-15	2000	3E	6-15	2000
	4E	8-15	1600	4E	8-12	1000
	5E	8-15	1600	5E	8-11	800
	6E	6-15	2000	6E	6-11	1200
	1W	13-15	600	1W		0
	2W	12-15	800	2W		0
	3W	12-15	800	3W	12-13	400
	4W	12-13	400	4W	12-13	400
	5W	12-13	400	5W	12-13	400
			Total 12,200			Total 8200
Markham	2	6-10	1000	2	6-10	1000
	3	6-20	2000	3	11-12	200
	4	1-5, 11-20	3000	4	1-5, 11-15, 19	2200
	5	1-5, 16-20	2000	5	1-5, 16-20	2000
	6	1-5, 11-15	2000	6	1-5, 11-15	2000
	7	1-5, 14-15	1400	7	1	200
	8	1-10	2000	8		0
			Total 13,400			Total 7600
Mississauga	2NDS	1-5, 11-23, 31-5	4600	2NDS	1-5, 11-23, 31-5	4600
	1E	1-10	2000	1E	1-5	1000
	1W	1-10	2000	1W	1-5	1000
	2W	1-12	2400	2	1-5	1000
	3W	1-12	2400	3	1-5, 11-12	1400
	4W	11-12	400	4	11-12	400
	5W	6-12	1400	5	6-12	1400
	6W	1-13	2600	6	1-13	2600
	10	1-10	2000	10	1-10	2000
	11	1-10	2000	11	1-10	2000
			Total 21,800			Total 17,400
Pickering	1	15-30	3000	1	15-30	3000

TABLE 1 cont'd

City or Town	Full Sample			Restricted sample		
	Conces-sion	Lots	Acres	Conces-sion	Lots	Acres
Richmond Hill	1W	41-5	1000	1W	41-5	1000
	1E	36-43, 51-3	2200	1E	36-43, 51-3	2200
	2E	11-26	3200	2E	11-26	3200
	3E	11-20	1000	3E	11-12	200
		Total	7400		Total	6600
Vaughan	1	26-35	2000	1	26-35	2000
	2	1-15	3000	2	1-10	2000
	3	1-15	3000	3	1-5	1000
	6	1-12	2400	6	2-8, 11-12	1800
	7	1-5, 11-12	1400	7	4-5	400
	8	1-10	2000	8	6-10	1000
		Total	13,800		Total	8200
Totals		Full sample	71,600		Restricted sample	48,300

us that the costs of assembling such parcels into a size sufficient for subdivision are prohibitive provided that larger parcels are available in the same area. This latter condition will certainly be satisfied for at least the next twenty years. Parcels under two acres can be divided by the severance process which circumvents the red tape of subdivision. Such severances are becoming increasingly hard to obtain, however, and were always hard to obtain for very small parcels. In any case, a large proportion of land held in parcels under two acres consists of single family houses on large lots (one half to one acre) that are unlikely to be divided for future housing units. Acreage figures resulting from the subtraction of all holdings under two acres will henceforth be referred to as net acres. Finally, acreage held as commercial or industrial property was eliminated with resulting figures that will be referred to as *net net* acres.

On this basis, nominal ownership figures were compiled using both the full and the restricted samples for the entire sample area and for each of the six towns individually. Net net acres in the full sample were 48,313.3 versus 34,272.5 in the restricted sample. The size of these figures relative to future development needs can be judged by CMHC figures which estimated residential land requirements for the Toronto region for the period 1971-80 at 19,600 acres for the Toronto Census Metropolitan area (considerably larger than our sample area). Other estimates range as high as 25,691 for the same period, while the

Spurr report estimates 3781 acres per year beginning in 1972. It is not, of course, being suggested that all development in the next ten or fifteen years will occur in our sample area. Some will occur on some remaining undeveloped land inside our sample area (e.g., Scarborough), and some will occur outside (e.g., Newmarket).

OWNERSHIP RESULTS

Sample results for nominal ownership in the entire sample area are shown in Tables 2A and 2B which list the top twenty-five owners in the full and restricted sample area, respectively. Tables 3 (A and B) through Tables 8 (A and B) show the top holdings for the individual municipalities. Since all of the Pickering land is included in the restricted sample, the table is not reproduced for the restricted sample. It is evident from these results that most of the large landowners are corporations or private companies registered in the land development business, which is not to say that they necessarily do any actual development. Although much of this land is actively farmed at present, little is owned by farmers, the overwhelming portion being rented or leased to farmers by the developer or holding company. Smaller holdings not listed on the table show an increasing proportion of individual (i.e., non-firm) owners, but a sizeable proportion of these smaller holdings are held by companies who own only a single parcel of 100 acres or less.[6] (These companies may, of course, own land outside the sample area.) The total number of companies that held land in the sample and were registered as being in the land development business numbered about 300.

Individual ownership of land accounted for no more than 25 per cent of the land in the full sample and significantly less in the restricted sample. With approximately ten exceptions, these individuals do not own enough land to generate even moderate ($10,000) levels of income from farming while even the poorest land in the sample from a developer's point of view could probably fetch $10,000 per acre. Thus an individual owning 100 acres, who could realize nowhere near $10,000 per year from farming, faces an opportunity cost of $1,000,000 (before taxes) or an income stream of $100,000 per year if invested

---

6 A finding given by Muller (1976) is that 25 per cent of all housing units approved for subdivision between January 1973 and July 1975 were connected with firms whose total approvals amounted to less than 200 units. A full 50 per cent of all approvals were connected with firms whose total approvals were less than 500 units. Figuring that in most cases these approved plans call for a density of at least four units to the acre, it is clear that a large amount of development does originate from land holdings of less than 150 acres.

TABLE 2A

Nominal ownership – full sample[1]

Rank	Company	Acres	Cumulative Acres	% of net net acres
1	Cadillac	3603.1		
2	Markborough	1856.8	Top 4	
3	Bramalea	1778.0		
4	Focal	1203.5	8441.4	17.5
5	Glen Ash	984.9	Top 6	
6	McLaughlin	899.4	10,325.7	21.4
7	Cedarland	888.7		
8	Developmental	824.2	Top 10	
9	Wimpey	673.5		
10	Pinetree	651.4	13,367.5	27.7
11	Goodman, M.	568.1		
12	Consolidated	525.6		
13	Monarch	502.8	Top 15	
14	Maple Wayn	408.3		
15	Langport	401.6	15,769.9	32.6
16	Great Thunder	395.2		
17	Runnymede	392.2		
18	Blechman et al.	375.2	Top 20	
19	Acumen	375.0		
20	Rindor	363.1	17,674.4	36.6
21	Harris, D. & W.	356.7		
22	Forest Glen	352.0		
23	Captain	338.7	Top 25	
24	Archway	337.5		
25	J.D.S.	307.0	19,366.3	40.1

1 Gross acres 71,600.0; net acres 57,862.5; net net acres 48,313.3.

at a 10 per cent rate of return. It is, therefore, fairly reasonable to conclude that most of this land held by individuals is held explicitly for speculative reasons and does in fact represent a competitive source of raw land to the large developers. It cannot be suggested that our net net acreage figures on which we calculate concentration are much of an overestimate of the true universe due to the prevalence of farmers who would not wish to sell their land.

The most obvious difficulty with this analysis of nominal ownership is that it overlooks possible linkages among companies. Popular opinion among planners, realtors, and developers themselves are that these linkages are quite common. The problems involved in establishing linkages are, however, substantial, involving both arriving at a definition of a linkage and then obtaining the data on whether or not a linkage exists. Given that many of the companies involved are

TABLE 2B

Nominal ownership – restricted sample[1]

Rank	Company	Acres	Cumulative Acres	% of net net acres
1	Cadillac	3603.1		
2	Markborough	1856.8	Top 4	
3	Bramalea	1778.0		
4	Focal	1092.1	8330.0	24.3
5	Glen Ash	885.5	Top 6	
6	Cedarland	888.7	10,104.2	29.5
7	Developmental	824.2		
8	McLaughlin	795.6	Top 10	
9	Goodman, M.	568.1		
10	Consolidated	525.6	12,817.7	37.4
11	Monarch	502.8		
12	Wimpey	471.2		
13	Pinetree	447.2	Top 15	
14	Langport	401.6		
15	Runnymede	392.2	15,032.7	43.9
16	Blechman et al.	375.2		
17	Acumen	375.0		
18	Rindor	363.1	Top 20	
19	Forest Glen	352.0		
20	Captain	338.7	16,836.7	49.1
21	Archway	337.5		
22	Markham 18-20	284.2		
23	Sander	270.1	Top 25	
24	J.D.S.	268.4		
25	Daniels et al.	262.4	18,259.3	53.3

1 Gross acres 48,300.0; net acres 40,422.5; net net acres 34.272.5.

privately owned and that several others are owned by foreign companies (e.g., Monarch), we decided to try to establish linkages by overlaps in principal officers and directors rather than by the seemingly impossible task of tracing links in equity ownership. It is interesting to note that this method of linking via officers and directors did show clear linkages in all the cases where we had *a priori* knowledge of links in equity ownership (Cadillac-Don Mills, Markborough-Wimpey, S.B. McLaughlin-Focal).

One individual sitting on the board of directors of each of the two companies need not imply joint decision-making between the two companies. It is not uncommon, for example, for a representative of a large bank to be placed on the board of directors of more than one company in the same industry when the

TABLE 3A

Brampton nominal ownership – full sample[1]

Rank	Company	Acres	Cumulative Acres	% of net net acres
1	Bramalea	1493.1		
2	Developmental	824.2	Top 4	
3	Wimpey	674.2		
4	Consolidated	525.6	3517.1	36.9
5	Maple Wayn	408.3	Top 6	
6	Markborough	307.7	4233.1	44.4
7	Amex	202.3	Top 10	
8	Sheard, W.	200.0		
9	Showcase	200.0		
10	Armstrong	172.6	5008.0	52.6

1 Gross acres 12,200.0; net acres 10,786.0; net net acres 9529.6.

TABLE 3B

Brampton nominal ownership – restricted sample[1]

Rank	Company	Acres	Cumulative Acres	% of net net acres
1	Bramalea	1493.1		
2	Developmental	824.2	Top 4	
3	Consolidated	525.6		50.4
4	Wimpey	471.2	3314.1	
5	Markborough	307.7	Top 6	
6	Amex	202.3	3824.1	58.1
7	Showcase	200.0		
8	Armstrong	172.6	Top 10	
9	Gdynia	138.1		
10	Batson	129.1	4463.9	67.9

1 Gross acres 8200.0; net acres 7471.2; net net acres 6578.5.

TABLE 4A

Markham nominal ownership – full sample[1]

Rank	Company	Acres	Cumulative acres	% of net net acres
1	Cedarland	888.7	Top 4	
2	Monarch	502.8		
3	Great Thunder	395.2		
4	Forest Glen	352.0	2138.7	26.7
5	Gold Lease Holds	250.0	Top 6	
6	Village Securities	242.1	2630.8	32.9
7	Schickedanz	194.8	Top 10	
8	J.D.S.	177.7		
9	Angus Glen	163.3		
10	Coniferous	152.9	3319.5	41.5

1 Gross acres 13,400.0; net acres 10,564.6; net net acres 7997.2.

TABLE 4B

Markham nominal ownership – restricted sample[1]

Rank	Company	Acres	Cumulative acres	% of net net acres
1	Cedarland	888.7		
2	Monarch	502.8	Top 4	
3	Forest Glen	352.0		
4	Village Securities	242.1	1985.6	47.4
5	Schickendanz	194.8	Top 6	
6	J.D.S.	177.7	2358.1	56.3
7	Settle	143.2	Top 10	
8	Morfrank	100.1		
9	Costain	97.0		
10	Seagram, E.	96.0	2794.4	66.7

1 Gross acres 7600.0; net acres 5579.5; net net acres 4188.8.

TABLE 5A

Mississauga nominal ownership — full sample[1]

Rank	Company	Acres	Cumulative acres	% of net net acres
1	Cadillac	3305.5	Top 4	
2	Markborough	1549.1		
3	Focal	1203.5		
4	S.B. McLaughlin	899.4	6957.5	40.2
5	Goodman, M.	568.1	Top 6	
6	Rindor	363.1	7888.7	45.6
7	Harris, D. & W.	356.2	Top 10	
8	Archway	337.5		
9	Daniels, J.	243.0		
10	Don Mills	209.1	9034.5	52.2

1 Gross acres 21,800.0; net acres 18,491.4; net net acres 17,291.9.

TABLE 5B

Mississauga nominal ownership — restricted sample[1]

Rank	Company	Acres	Cumulative acres	% of net net acres
1	Cadillac	3305.5		
2	Markborough	1549.1	Top 4	
3	Focal	1092.1		
4	S.B. McLaughlin	795.6	6742.3	51.4
5	Goodman, M.	568.1	Top 6	
6	Rindor	363.1	7673.5	58.5
7	Archway	337.5		
8	Daniels, S.J.	243.0	Top 10	
9	Don Mills	209.1		
10	Cinderhill	199.2	8663.2	66.0

1 Gross acres 17,400.0; net acres 14,182.9; net net acres 13,127.3.

TABLE 6

Pickering nominal ownership – full sample[1]

Rank	Company	Acres	Cumulative acres	% of net net acres
1	Bramalea	284.9	Top 4	
2	Runnymede	242.9		
3	J.D.S.	90.7		
4	Dunbar, J.	83.8	702.3	66.8

1 Gross acres 3,000.0; net acres 1,281.4; net net acres 1,051.7.

TABLE 7A

Richmond Hill nominal ownership – full sample[1]

Rank	Company	Acres	Cumulative acres	% of net net acres
1	Glen Ash	485.0	Top 4	
2	Markham	284.2		
3	Captain	270.4		
4	Sander	270.1	1309.7	32.3
5	Atura	186.3	Top 6	
6	Macartney, G.	145.1	1641.1	40.5

1 Gross acres 7400.0; net acres 5500.6; net net acres 4055.0.

TABLE 7B

Richmond Hill nominal ownership – restricted sample[1]

Rank	Company	Acres	Cumulative acres	% of net net acres
1	Glen Ash	485.0	Top 4	
2	Markham 18-20	284.2	1309.8	37.1
3	Captain	270.4		
4	Sander	270.1		
5	Atura	186.3	Top 6	
6	Strasser, A.	128.0	1724.0	46.0

1 Gross acres 6600.0; net acres 4975.3; net net acres 3529.9.

TABLE 8A

Vaughan nominal ownership – full sample[1]

Rank	Company	Acres	Cumulative acres	% of net net acres
1	Glen Ash	499.9		
2	Pinetree	437.4	Top 4	
3	Langport	401.6		
4	Blechman, G.	375.2	1714.1	20.4
5	Acumen	375.0	Top 6	
6	Rexdale	233.3	2322.4	27.7
7	Woodfield	220.3	Top 10	
8	Revenue Properties	214.4		
9	Pasquale, E.	212.2		
10	Baker Farms	198.6	3167.9	37.8

1 Gross acres 13,800.0; net acres 11,238.5; net net acres 8,387.9.

TABLE 8B

Vaughan nominal ownership – restricted sample[1]

Rank	Company	Acres	Cumulative acres	% of net net acres
1	Pinetree	437.4	Top 4	
2	Langport	401.6		
3	Glen Ash	400.5		
4	Blechman, G.	375.2	1614.7	27.9
5	Acumen	375.0	Top 6	
6	Revenue Properties	214.4	2204.1	38.0
7	Algonquin	182.6	Top 10	
8	Costain	139.4		
9	Gravina, D.	127.4		
10	Bond Street	120.9	2774.4	47.9

1 Gross acres 8200.0; net acres 6997.7; net net acres 5796.3.

bank has large financial commitments to each firm. Such a director may be interested only in the financial solvency of each company and may have no knowledge of the day-to-day business activities which may bring the two firms into competition. Representatives of large law firms often sit on boards of directors for similar reasons. The question of collusion implied by shared directors is not black and white, however. At the one extreme of collusive

TABLE 9

Major composite companies – Level I linkages (listed by size)

Rank	Composite components	Full sample acreage	Linkages
1	Cadillac	3603.1	Principal officers and
	Don Mills	209.1	boards of directors
		Total 3812.2	share 5 members
2	Bramalea	1778.0	Principal officers and
	Developmental	824.2	boards of directors
		Total 2602.2	share 2 members
3	Markborough	1856.8	Principal officers and
	Wimpey	673.5	boards of directors
		Total 2530.3	share 2 members
4	S.B. McLaughlin	899.4	Principle officers and
	Focal	1203.4	boards of directors
		Total 2102.9	share 7 members
5	Cedarland	888.7	Principal officers and
	Bond St.	120.9	boards of directors
	Coventry	98.1	share a minimum of
	Duff-Von	89.3	1 member and a maximum
	Fiston	27.0	of 2 members
	Gdynia	138.0	
	Liverton	35.3	
	N.H.D.	189.5	
	Thicket	11.1	
	Vondale	7.6	
	Glen Cove	102.7	
	Village Securities	242.1	
		Total 1950.3	
6	Pinetree	641.4	Principal officers and
	Runnymede	392.2	boards of directors share a
	Woodfield	220.3	minimum of 1 member and a maximum
	F.T. Development	11.3	of 2 members. Acreage listed
	Rexdale	233.3	under Max Tannenbaum (associated
	Max Tannenbaum	181.4	with Pinetree, F.T. Dev., and Woodfield)
		Total 1689.9	is privately held
7	Glen Ash	984.9	Glen Ash is not a company but a
	Carvil[1]	68.3	style name of a consortium made
		Total 1053.2	up of Carvil Enterprises,
			Garthorne Investments, and
			Whitland Construction
8	Consolidated	525.6	Principal officers and
	Archway	337.5	boards of directors
		Total 863.1	share 1 member

1 Acreage owned jointly by Glen Ash and Carvil is listed only in the total for Glen Ash.

TABLE 9 cont'd

Rank	Composite components	Full sample acreage	Linkages
9	Acumen	375.0	Principal officers and
	Arrandene	105.9	boards of directors
	East Woodbridge	62.7	share 3 members except for
	Loon	2.5	Rayland Investments which
	Rayland	100.9	shares only 1 member with the
	West Woodbridge	72.3	others
	Gasmuz	10.1	
		Total 729.4	
10	Sander	270.1	Principal officers and
	Atura	186.3	boards of directors
	Milestar	76.9	share 1 member
		Total 533.3	
11	Coniferous	152.9	Principal officers and
	Cupra	100.0	boards of directors
	Settle	143.2	share 2 members
		Total 396.1	
12	J.D.S.	307.0	Principal officers and
	North Keele[2]	26.7	boards of directors
		Total 333.7	share 2 members

2 Acreage owned jointly by J.D.S. and North Keele is listed only in the total for J.D.S.

behaviour are two companies that behave as one company, maximizing joint profits. In response to the question of why two firms in that position would not simply merge, some would argue that it is easier to do business (particularly buying of land) if the company appears to be small than if it is recognized as a large developer. At the other end of the spectrum, a director may only be a member of a large bank there to ensure solvency as just mentioned. Situations between these two extremes may be more likely. Minor day-to-day decisions which may bring the two firms in which an individual is a director into competition may be carried out without the knowledge of that director. Larger decisions, however, such as the decision to buy and assemble several hundred acres for development involve millions of dollars and are quite unlikely to be undertaken without the knowledge of all members of the board. If this is true, it seems unlikely that the director of two different companies would ever allow the two firms to bid competitively against one another for the same piece of land. This type of argument suggests that firms sharing only one director are likely to avoid competition between themselves that is highly detrimental to the joint maximization of profits. We have, therefore, decided to link companies which share one or more principal officers or members of the boards of directors. We have termed such linkages level I linkages and the resulting composite companies are shown in Table 9. It should be noted that the principal officers and directors of the top four resulting composite companies share at least 2 members.

Composite company rankings and concentration figures for all towns combined are shown in Tables 10A and 10B for the full and restricted samples, respectively. Similarly, figures for the individual towns are shown in Tables 11 (A and B) through 15 (A and B). Since the linkages produced no increased concentration in Pickering, Table 6 is not reproduced.

More tenuous linkages among companies have also been compiled. These linkages occur when two companies are linked through an officer or director of a third company or an even longer chain of companies. The only significant example of such linkages involves the composite companies listed in Table 9 as Cedarland, Pinetree, Acumen, together with a number of other companies. This linkage pattern is shown in Table 16. Cedarland shares at least one officer or director with each company in the second column. Companies in the third column share at least one officer or director with the corresponding company in the second column, but share no one with Cedarland, and so forth. Companies like Cedarland and Pinetree are shown as linked on the third level, hence the term level III linkages. Level III linkages for the entire sample area are shown in Tables 17A and 17B. Concentration figures for individual towns at level III are not significantly higher than at level I, except in the case of Vaughan where the top 4 own 41 and 52 per cent of full and restricted samples, respectively, at level III linkage.

The level of linkages which should be adopted in measuring market concentration is not clear. It is, perhaps, reasonable to adopt the position that any level I linkage between two companies will at very least lead those two companies to avoid the type of costly competition mentioned above. It is not at all clear that this proposition is generally valid for level III linkages. Cedarland and Pinetree, for example, are linked through a rather long chain of individuals. Cedarland shares one individual with Glen Cove which shares a different individual with Runnymede. Runnymede, in turn, shares a third person with Pinetree who is not involved with either Glen Cove or Cedarland. It is possible that costly competition may be avoided by passing information along this chain but this would seem to be less efficient than outright collusion. The issue of whether or not there is collusion in the market is different from the issue of whether or not there is market concentration. The issue of collusion will be treated later on in this chapter. For discussions of market concentration *per se*, it is our feeling that companies linked at the second or third level should not be treated as a single company. It is probably reasonable, however, to treat companies linked at level I as a single company, even if the linkage consists only of one shared director. The confidence in level I linkages obviously does increase if more than one person is shared by the two companies or if the one person shared is a principal officer of both companies rather than a director.

It is worth noting that equally difficult problems would arise if we had linked companies on the basis of equity ownership. If one individual owned 20 per cent of each of two companies, for example, can it be concluded that the two companies behave as if they were maximizing joint profits? If this were the only ownership overlap, the answer would likely be no, since joint profit maximization would likely imply losses for the other stockholders of one (but not both) of the companies relative to a more competitive position. It could, however, probably be argued that such an overlap might prevent the firms from bidding against one another in the manner outlined above. But even this type of co-ordination would require that our stockholder in question take an active interest in the company.

Returning to the data, several interesting results are immediately apparent. First, the concentration figures for the entire sample area are very much lower than the figures for all of the individual towns, implying that developers tend to stick 'close to home.' This result was true in both the full and the restricted samples and for both nominal and effective ownership. In the nominal ownership restricted sample, for example, the top 10 firms own 37.4 per cent of the land, while the *lowest* figure for an individual is 47.9 per cent for Vaughan. Figures of at least 66 per cent are registered for Brampton, Markham, Mississauga, and Pickering. There are obvious advantages to a firm concentrating in one town, such as minimizing the number of government units with which the developer must deal. Developers have asserted to us in interviews that a major component of a developer's value added in land development is moving the sub-division application through the various levels of government red tape. A major portion of this process occurs at the municipal and regional government levels. The sub-division application at the local level, for example, must be negotiated, revised, and renegotiated with a number of offices such as the planning department, works department, board of education, health department, parks and recreation, planning board, and town council. It would seem that for a fixed amount of development activity, a company can possibly realize significant savings by dealing with only one municipality. The reader should note at this point that the delineation of subsets of land by political boundaries is not necessarily appropriate. An appropriate delineation would define relevant market areas. We will return to this point in our later discussion of the concentration ratios.

Comparing the data on nominal ownership to those on effective ownership, we found that affiliated companies tended to operate in the same towns or

TABLE 10A

Level I effective ownership – full sample (net net acres 48,313.3

Rank	Composite company	Acres	Cumulative acres	% of net net acres	Similar % for nominal ownership
1	Cadillac	3812.2			
2	Bramalea	2602.2	Top 4		
3	Markborough	2530.3			
4	S.B. McLaughlin	2102.9	11,047.6[1]	22.7	17.5
5	Cedarland	1950.3	Top 6		
6	Pinetree	1689.9	14,685.8	30.5	21.4
7	Glen Ash	1053.2			
8	Consolidated	863.1	Top 10		
9	Acumen	729.4			
10	Goodman, M.	568.1	17,899.6	37.1	27.7
11	Sander	533.3			
12	Monarch	502.8	Top 15		
13	Maple Wayn	408.3			
14	Langport	401.6			
15	Coniferous	396.1	20,141.7	41.7	32.6
16	Great Thunder	395.2			
17	Blechman, et al.	375.2	Top 20		
18	Rindor	363.1			
19	Harris, D. and W.	356.7			
20	Forest Glen	352.0	21,983.9	45.5	36.6
21	Captain	338.7			
22	J.D.S.	333.7	Top 25		
23	Alliance	303.7			
24	Costain	286.4			
25	Markham 18-20	284.2	23,529.6[2]	48.7	40.1

1 There is a double counting of 32.9 acres jointly owned by Don Mills (part of the Cadillac composite) and Markborough.

2 A double counting of 68.3 acres is due to a joint ownership by North Keele (part of the J.D.S. composite) and Runnymede (part of the Pinetree composite). Total double counting affects concentration figures by less than .1%.

TABLE 10B

Level I effective ownership – restricted sample (net net acres 34,272.5)

Rank	Composite company	Acres	Cumulative acres[1]	% of net net acres	Similar % for nominal ownership
1	Cadillac	3812.2	Top 4		
2	Bramalea	2602.2			
3	Markborough	2328.0			
4	S.B. McLaughlin	1887.7	10,630.1	31.0	24.3
5	Cedarland	1863.4	Top 6		
6	Pinetree	1265.4	13,758.9	40.1	29.5
7	Glen Ash	953.8	Top 10		
8	Consolidated	863.1			
9	Acumen	694.8			
10	Goodman, M.	568.1	16,838.7	49.1	37.4
11	Monarch	502.8			
12	Sander	456.4	Top 15		
13	Langport	401.6			
14	Blechman, et al.	375.2			
15	Rindor	363.1	18,937.8	55.3	43.9
16	Forest Glen	352.0			
17	Captain	338.7	Top 20		
18	Markham 18-20	284.2			
19	J.D.S.	268.4			
20	Daniels et al.	262.4	20,443.5	59.6	49.1
21	Coniferous	243.2			
22	Village Sec.	242.1			
23	Costain	236.4			
24	Batsen	219.0			
25	Revenue Prop.	214.4	21,598.6	63.0	53.3

1 The same double count noted in footnotes 1 and 2 following Table 10A occurs here. Total double counting affects concentration figures by less than .1%.

TABLE 11A

Brampton level I effective ownership – full sample (net net acres 9529.6)

Rank	Composite company	Acres	Cumulative acres	% of net net acres	Similar % for nominal ownership
1	Bramalea	2317.3			
2	Markborough	981.2	Top 4		
3	Maple Wayn[1]	644.5			
4	Consolidated	525.6	4468.6	46.9	36.9
5	Amex	202.3	Top 6		
6	Sheard, W.	200.0	4870.9	51.1	44.4
7	Showcase	200.0			
8	Armstrong	172.6	Top 10		
9	Hewson, J.	153.8			
10	Batson	129.1	5526.4	58.0	52.6

1 Consists of Coventry, Maple Wayn, and Gdynia

TABLE 11B

Brampton level I effective ownership – restricted sample (net net acres 6578.5)

Rank	Composite company	Acres	Cumulative acres	% of net net acres	Similar % for nominal ownership
1	Bramalea	2317.3			
2	Markborough	778.9	Top 4		
3	Consolidated	525.6			
4	Maple Wayn	359.2	3,981.0	60.5	50.4
5	Amex	202.3	Top 6		
6	Showcase	200.0	4,383.3	66.6	58.1
7	Armstrong	172.6			
8	Batson	129.1	Top 10		
9	Heart Lake	128.9			
10	Silver Rose	122.6	4,936.5	75.0	67.9

TABLE 12A

Markham level I effective ownership – full sample (net net acres 7997.2)

Rank	Composite company	Acres	Cumulative acres	% of net net acres	Similar % for nominal ownership
1	Cedarland	1157.8	Top 4		
2	Monarch	502.8			
3	Coniferous	396.1			
4	Great Thunder	395.2	2451.9	30.7	26.7
5	Forest Glen	352.0	Top 6		
6	Gold Lease Hold	250.0	3053.9	38.2	32.9
7	Schikedanz	194.8			
8	J.D.S.	177.7	Top 10		
9	Angus Glen	163.3			
10	Costain	147.0	3736.7	46.7	41.5

TABLE 12B

Markham level I effective ownership – restricted sample (net net acres 4188.8)

Rank	Composite company	Acres	Cumulative acres	% of net net acres	Similar % for nominal ownership
1	Cedarland	1157.8	Top 4		
2	Monarch	502.8			
3	Forest Glen	352.0			
4	Coniferous	243.2	2255.8	53.9	47.4
5	Schikedanz	194.8	Top 6		
6	J.D.S.	177.7	2628.3	62.7	56.3
7	Morfrank	100.0	Top 10		
8	Costain	97.0			
9	Seagram, E.	96.0			
10	Erinview	69.9	2991.3	71.4	66.7

TABLE 13A

Mississauga level I effective ownership – full sample (net net acres 17,291.9)

Rank	Composite company	Acres	Cumulative acres	% of net net acres	Similar % for nominal ownership
1	Cadillac	3514.6			
2	S.B. McLaughlin	2102.9	Top 4		
3	Markborough	1549.1			
4	Goodman, M.	568.1	7734.7	44.7	40.2
5	Pinetree	466.6	Top 6		
6	Rindor	363.1	8564.4	49.5	45.6
7	Harris, D. and W.	356.2			
8	Archway	337.5	Top 10		
9	Daniels, J.	243.0			
10	Cinderhill	199.2	9700.3	56.1	52.2

TABLE 13B

Mississauga level I effective ownership – restricted sample (net net acres 13,127.3)

Rank	Composite company	Acres	Cumulative acres	% of net net acres	Similar % for nominal ownership
1	Cadillac	3514.6	Top 4		
2	S.B. McLaughlin	1887.7			
3	Markborough	1549.1			
4	Goodman, M.	568.1	7419.5	56.5	51.4
5	Rindor	363.1	Top 6		
6	Archway	337.5	8120.1	61.9	58.4
7	Pinetree	262.4			
8	Daniels, S.J.	243.0	Top 10		
9	Cinderhill	199.2			
10	Cordingley, M. and J.	150.2	8974.9	68.4	66.0

TABLE 14A

Richmond Hill level I effective ownership – full sample (net net acres 4055.0)

Rank	Composite company	Acres	Cumulative acres	% of net net acres	Similar % for nominal ownership
1	Glen Ash	485.0			
2	Sander	456.0	Top 4		
3	Markham 18-20	284.2			
4	Captain	270.4	1496.0	36.9	32.3
5	Macartney, G.	145.1	Top 6		
6	Stasser, A.	128.0	1769.1	43.6	40.5

TABLE 14B

Richmond Hill level I effective ownership – restricted sample (net net acres 3529.9)

Rank	Composite company	Acres	Cumulative acres	% of net net acres	Similar % for nominal ownership
1	Glen Ash	485.0			
2	Sander	456.4	Top 4		
3	Markham 18-20	284.2			
4	Captain	270.4	1496.0	42.4	37.1
5	Strasser, A.	128.0	Top 6		
6	Watford, M.	100.0	1724.0	48.8	46.0

TABLE 15A

Vaughan level I effective ownership – full sample (net net acres 8387.9)

Rank	Composite company	Acres	Cumulative acres	% of net net acres	Similar % for nominal ownership
1	Pinetree	959.3	Top 4		
2	Acumen	729.4			
3	Glen Ash	568.2			
4	Cedarland	401.8	2658.7	31.7	20.4
5	Langport	401.6	Top 6		
6	Blechman, et al.	375.2	3435.5	41.0	27.7
7	Revenue Properties	214.4			
8	Pasquale, E.	212.2	Top 10		
9	Baker Frams	198.6			
10	Algonquin	182.6	4243.3	50.6	37.8

TABLE 15B

Vaughan level I effective ownership – restricted sample (net net acres 5796.3)

Rank	Composite company	Acres	Cumulative acres	% of net net acres	Similar % for nominal ownership
1	Pinetree	739.0			
2	Acumen	694.8	Top 4		
3	Glen Ash	468.8			
4	Langport	401.8	2304.2	39.8	27.9
5	Blechman, et al.	375.2	Top 6		
6	Cedarland	323.9	3003.3	51.8	38.0
7	Algonquin	182.6			
8	Costain	139.4	Top 10		
9	Gravina, D.	127.4			
10	Homes Dev.	107.0	3559.7	61.4	47.9

TABLE 16

Level III linkages – the Cedarland-Pinetree complex[1]

Cedarland (888.7) –	Bond St. (120.9) –	Acumen (375.0)		
		Arrandene (105.9)		
		E. Woodbridge (62.7)		
		Richmond Hill (25.5) –	Loon (2.5)	
		Gasmuz (0)	Rayland (100.9)	
		W. Woodbridge (72.3)		
	Coventry (98.1) –	Maple Wayne (408.3)		
	Duff-Von (89.3) –	Mississauga 14 (30.4)		
		Treeford (89.2)		
	Glen Cove (102.7) –	Rexdale (233.3)	Pinetree (651.4)	
		Runnymede (392.5) –	Woodfield (220.3)	
			F.T. Development (11.3)	
			M. Tannenbaum (181.4)	
	Fiston (27.0)			
	Gdynia (138.0)			
	Jan-Sil (0) –	Golden-B (10.0)		
	Liverton (35.3)			
	N.H.D. (189.5) –	Park Forest (3.0)		
		Tordale (50.0)		
	Thicket (11.1)			
	Vondale (7.6) –	Cogan (57.5)		
	Village (242.1)			

1 Acreage in parentheses

TABLE 17A

Level III effective ownership – full sample (net net acres 48,313.3)

Rank	Composite company	Acres	Cumulative acres	% of net net acres	Similar % for nominal ownership
1	Cedarland-Pinetree	5033.4	Top 4		
2	Cadillac	3812.2			
3	Bramalea	2602.2			
4	Markborough	2530.3	13,978.1	28.9	17.5
5	S.B. McLaughlin	2102.9	Top 6		
6	Glen Ash	1053.2	17,134.2	35.7	21.4
7	Consolidated	863.1			
8	Goodman, M.	568.1	Top 10		
9	Sander	533.3			
10	Monarch	502.8	18,601.5	40.6	27.7

TABLE 17B

Level III effective ownership – restricted sample (net net acres 34,272.5)

Rank	Composite company	Acres	Cumulative acres	% of net net acres	Similar % for nominal ownership
1	Cedarland-Pinetree	4092.6	Top 4		
2	Cadillac	3812.2			
3	Bramalea	2602.2			
4	Markborough	2328.0	12,835.0	37.4	24.3
5	S.B. McLaughlin	1887.0	Top 6		
6	Glen Ash	953.8	15,675.0	45.7	29.5
7	Consolidated	863.1			
8	Goodman, M.	568.1	Top 10		
9	Monarch	502.8			
10	Sander	456.4	18,066.2	52.7	37.4

regional municipalities (Mississauga and Brampton are in Peel; Markham, Richmond Hill, and Vaughan are in York; Pickering is in Durham). Among the top 4 composite companies given in Table 9. Cadillac was concentrated in Mississauga, Bramalea in Brampton, Markborough in Brampton and Mississauga (Peel), and S.B. McLaughlin in Mississauga. This result makes the issue of joint decision-making within each composite company more important since it does seem that the companies would come into competition in the course of normal business activity.

Another result that occurred in the entire sample area and in all of the individual towns was that concentration in the restricted sample was significantly higher than the concentration in the full sample. Nominal ownership statistics for holdings of the top 4 developers in the entire sample area jump from 17.5 per cent to 24.3 per cent, for example. Similar statistics for level I effective ownership jump from 22.7 per cent to 31.0 per cent. On average, the increase in top 4 concentration jumped just about 33 per cent in the individual towns. Not only was concentration low in the land eliminated from the full sample (as described above), but the bigger developers were seldom among the owners of the land. In a static sense, this means that land nearer to development is more likely to be held by the larger developers. In a dynamic sense, it suggests that land is traded up from farmers to speculators and then from speculators to developers as the time for development approaches. This suggests that much if not most of the risk bearing on land is done by small developers and speculators. This is particularly true in the unzoned land eliminated from the full sample to form the restricted sample.

In order to assess the likelihood of the existence of market power in the Toronto area we must draw on the analysis in chapter 2. In that chapter we showed that market power would exist if the following two conditions hold: (1) there is significant concentration of ownership of land near the boundaries of current development; and (2) the growth rate of the urban area and the amount of 'developable' land are sufficient for the amount of this 'developable' land to be significant relative to the totality of 'developable' and developed land in the appropriately defined urban area. Earlier in this chapter we discussed various estimates of the amount of land necessary for future development needs for the Toronto area. It seems very likely that the Toronto area will grow enough to encompass roughly at least our restricted sample within twenty years, so condition (2) may hold. However, it is important to note that our concentration figures have a substantial upward bias, since we used the amount of land in our sample rather than the totality of 'developable' and developed land in the relevant area for our basis.

With this bias in mind we are now in a position to discuss whether or not sufficient concentration of ownership exists to suggest the existence of market power. Traditional statistics on market concentration have often looked at the holdings of the top four or six firms in the industry as a percentage of the total. Tables 10A and 10B show that the top four companies at level I effective ownership hold only 22.7 per cent and 31.0 per cent of the full and restricted sample acreage. The highest degree of concentration in an individual town is in Pickering where the top four hold 66 per cent. But this last figure is an exception and in any case amounts to only a small part of the entire sample area (e.g., our sample does not include the massive government land assembly in Pickering). The next highest level of top four concentration at level I of effective ownership occurs in Brampton where the top four own 46.9 per cent and 60.5 per cent of the full and the restricted samples respectively. The lowest level of effective ownership occurred in Vaughan where the top four only owned 31.7 per cent and 39.8 per cent of the full and restricted samples.

The concentration figures for the entire sample area are too low to imply market power by traditional industrial organization standards. This is true even at level III effective ownership where the top four own only 28.9 per cent and 37.4 per cent of the full and restricted samples respectively as shown in Tables 17A and 17B. While no industrial organization economist would like to be pinned down as to what sort of concentration implies market power and resource misallocation, holdings of less than 70 per cent by the top four has typically not generated accusations of market power on the basis of concentration alone. Except for the Pickering statistic just mentioned, the individual towns do not approach this figure even at level I effective ownership in the restricted sample where the figures range from 60.5 per cent in Brampton to 39.8 per cent in Vaughan. The figures for Brampton (60.5 per cent), Markham (53.9 per cent), and Mississauga (56.5 per cent) are not notably low, however (although they are biased upward by the definition of concentration ratio we have used), and so these municipalities will have to be discussed in more detail.

An alternate summary statistic on ownership concentration can be computed using the Herfindahl index of concentration. This index of concentration is computed by squaring the holdings of each firm as a percentage of the market and summing the resulting figures over all firms. The index ranges from 0 to 1, the former being an industry with many infinitely small firms and the latter being a complete monopoly. The Herfindahl index for level I effective ownership for the entire sample area is 0.019 and 0.035 for the full and the restricted samples respectively. For Brampton, which has the highest concentration in the effective ownership statistics except for the small sample in Pickering, the figures are 0.095 and 0.155 for the full and the restricted samples respectively. As was the case using concentration ratios, these figures are not in themselves sufficient to imply market power and resource misallocation.

Given the significant difference between the degree of concentration in the entire sample area and in the individual towns, an important question arises as to what geographic. domain is the appropriate one for measuring market power. While it is true that all areas in the sample are in the same commuter shed relative to the Metro core, there are a number of reasons why different locations in the sample area may not be good locational substitutes from the consumer's point of view. In other words, it may be that our sample area consists of a group of somewhat differentiated products. In this case the degree of differentiation (measured by cross elasticity of demand) determines how many separate markets there are.

The first reason why the sample area may not be perfectly homogeneous from the consumer's point of view is due to the fact that employment is not centralized in the Metro core, but spread out to a certain extent over the metro area. Important employment centres are located in Mississauga and along the highway 401 corridor for example. For those not familiar with the Toronto area, the 401 is a major trunk highway that runs east-west through the sample area, passing just south of the boundary between Metro Toronto on the one hand and the towns of Markham and Vaughan on the other. It then continues westward through the northeast corner of Mississauga and on into Brampton. Individuals whose employment is in Mississauga or along the western portion of the 401 corridor would certainly not be indifferent between a residential location in Mississauga or Brampton versus one in Markham, other things being equal. Individuals in this type of situation would tend to see locations in different towns as different products. If this type of individual dominated, the statistics for concentration in the individual towns might be more appropriate for assessing market power than the statistics for the area as a whole. On the other hand, there is a large concentration of employment in the Metro core and individuals having employment there would presumably be indifferent between locations with equal access, other things equal.

Other things are not, of course, generally equal. Levels of public services are one thing that can differ among municipalities. Per capita expenditures on schooling, for example, create a form of product differentiation in the eyes of households with school age children. Related to differences in public services are differences in municipal tax rates. Low tax rates are obviously attractive. Other types of characteristics which tend to differentiate different locations include such things as access to recreation areas. Lake Ontario is one pole to the south and the lake and ski areas to the north form another pole.

All of the above argue for the recognition of the fact that there is location differentiation within a fixed commuter shed to the central core. It is beyond the scope of this study to assess the extent to which this phenomenon reduces the cross elasticity of demand for land between the different locations. Perhaps the best that we can do is simply argue that the concentration statistics for the entire sample area are an underestimate of the 'ideal' measure of concentration and that the statistics for the individual towns are likely to be an overestimate of this measure. Notice, however, that the use of political boundaries to delineate subsets of land is probably not appropriate. This is because the municipalities do not form disjoint commuter sheds. (See Table 1.1 in Muller, 1976). That the results are sensitive to this delineation can be seen by the fact that if we aggregate adjoining municipalities (e.g., Brampton and Mississauga) the concentration ratios fall dramatically. Whatever the appropriate definition of market area for the short run, we would argue the long-run cross-elasticities of demand for land at different locations are very high, since production location decisions (and therefore employment centres) will certainly respond in the long run to land price differentiates.

Several final words are in order concerning the effect of the size and composition of our sample on the concentration figures. For a sample of the fixed size of ours, we feel that is highly unlikely that a different sample could be constructed in this commuter shed which would show significantly higher concentration. Our sample is not a random sample. It was carefully picked to include all the areas where development is most likely to take place and all areas where major land assembly has been known to take place. In this sense, the sample is biased in that it includes all large land holdings by the larger developers. Areas like Erin Mills and Meadowvale in Mississauga, for example, were deliberately included in the sample while adjacent areas in which planners asserted there were no large developers operating were left out (Erin Mills is a Cadillac development and Meadowvale is a Markborough development). We are not prepared, therefore, to entertain a suggestion that a different sample of the same size would yield higher concentration statistics.

Increasing the size of the sample would influence the results. We assert that increases in the size of the sample (e.g., by including land that cannot be serviced in the next five years) will decrease the observed level of concentration. This should be evident from our results in which concentration in the restricted sample was significantly higher than in the full sample. We would expect that land that is even less likely to be developed than that in the full sample would show an even lower concentration. Reducing the sample further until we are left with the land recently approved for subdivision, on the other hand, will raise the concentration figures somewhat as noted in the figures quoted from Muller (1976) earlier. But our chapter on the timing of land development emphasizes that this is a questionable procedure. That chapter argues that in a long-run competitive equilibrium, it is somewhat arbitrary as to who develops land in a given year, and that an observation that one developer has accounted for a significant proportion the development in one year may be consistent with a perfectly competitive market.

In the opinion of the authors, it *cannot* be concluded on the basis of the evidence on concentration that we have presented that exercised market is an important characteristic of the Toronto land market. We base this opinion on the data and our belief that the cross run elasticity of demand for land in adjoining municipalities is probably quite large.

BARRIERS TO ENTRY

Another common method used by industrial organization economists to assess market power is to analyse barriers to entry into the industry in question. Barriers to entry are defined differently by different economists but the most well-defined notion is that barriers to entry occur when new firms must face costs not faced by existing firms. It is not clear, however, what any of the traditional notions of barriers to entry have to do with the land market. The basic problem here is that the total supply of undeveloped land in the relevant area is fixed. No new firms can simply start up the business of land holding. A new firm cannot enter the industry under any circumstance except that of inducing an existing landowner to sell land and thereby withdraw from the industry. Existing landowners are, therefore, not threatened with entry. A collusive agreement to fix land prices by existing landowners is not threatened from the outside. Issues such as limit pricing to prevent entry do not arise. Collusive agreements to fix prices are, of course, always threatened from the inside, a topic which will be discussed in the next section.

Therefore, as we showed in chapter 2, barriers to entering the landowning business are absolute. This fact makes the ownership concentration figures discussed above take on a new significance, especially for the individual towns. In the effective ownership statistics, for example, the top four firms own 60.5 per cent of the restricted sample in Brampton (Table 11B) while the top ten own 75 per cent. The 25 per cent is distributed over a large number of landowners holding rather small acreage. A collusive agreement among the top ten firms could certainly lead to the existence of exercised market power (although again the basis used for the calculation of the concentration ratios gives them an upward bias), if the township is the relevant definition of the market area. Similar arguments can be made for the other municipalities in the sample.

The extent to which concentration of land ownership in Brampton or in any other municipality is meaningful in terms of resource misallocation still comes back to the question of to what extent consumers regard land in different municipalities as good substitutes. If consumers regard all land in the sample area as perfect substitutes, then it is meaningless to have a monopoly in Brampton if your holdings are only a small fraction of the total. Referring back to Tables 10A and 10B it is noted once again that concentration in the entire sample area is very much smaller than in the individual towns. Still, effective ownership statistics do show that the top ten firms own about 50 per cent of the restricted sample. About 30 firms and individuals are needed, however, to make up two-thirds of the market.

We conclude this section then by noting that if households regard land in different municipalities as very poor substitutes, then the high barriers to entry in the market suggest that there may be market power exercised in the land market at least in the short run, before production location decisions are influenced by land price differentials. If households regard land in different municipalities as good substitutes, however, the case for market power and resource misallocation is very weak despite the high barriers to entry. It must also be remembered that our sample is confined to a given commuting shed and that there is some undeveloped land closer in than our sample and an obviously vast amount of land outside the sample area. While much of this land further out cannot be serviced in the short run, it does represent a competing source of land in the longer run if land at 50 or 60 minutes commuting distance is a reasonably good substitute for land at 40 or 45 minutes commuting distance.

BARRIERS TO COLLUSION

It is well recognized that the extent to which an oligopolistic industry can distort prices away from the competitive levels depends upon its ability to behave in a collusive fashion. Many industrial organization economists argue that this ability essentially depends upon the ability of the industry to enforce a collusive agreement, since any such agreement creates strong incentives for any one member to deviate from that agreement. Ability to enforce the agreement, in turn, depends upon the ability of the firms in the industry to easily detect deviations from that agreement.

It would seem that the land market satisfies very well the condition that deviations from a collusive agreement are easily detected. First, since land transactions are subject to a provincial transfer tax, all transactors must report the true sale price under penalty of law. These sale prices are recorded at the registry and are freely available to any interested party. Second, the total number of transactions on land in a given time period is small in the sense that it would not be at all costly for any development company to observe all sales prices involving his competitors. Indeed, transactions on land and housing are published monthly for Metropolitan Toronto by TEELA market surveys. For both of these reasons it would be difficult for any collusive agreement by landowners to be threatened by secret price cutting.

The opposite side of the coin from sale price of land is quantity. The objective of collusion is ultimately not to restrict sales *per se* but to restrict over time (not necessarily in any one year as argued earlier) the amount of land that gets developed. Sales of land from one owner to another are not necessarily of interest to a cartel unless that sale is associated with increased development. Looking at things from this point of view it seems that the case for ease of collusion becomes stronger. Normally, we are thinking in terms of being able to detect violations of a pricing agreement *ex post*. But a decision by one firm to develop land faster than an agreed upon rate is now *ex ante* in the sense that the violation will be apparent as soon as the violating firm files a plan of subdivision, which is normally about two years before actual development begins. This leaves other firms a good deal of time to take counter actions which might leave the first firm in a very bad position indeed.

These arguments suggest that the ability of the development industry to sustain a collusive agreement is very strong. The problem of how to generate such a collusive agreement in the first place is not very different here than in any other industry. The problem is basically to arrive at some agreeable division of the market among the existing firms. This issue is well developed in the industrial organization literature and will not be treated here. It should be noted, however, that the dynamic nature of demand plus the fact that the stock of land is fixed means that market shares should be defined over a long period of time, say ten or twenty years. The fact that there are large fluctuations from year to year in the market shares of firms registering subdivisions or selling serviced lots must not be taken as evidence that a collusive agreement does not exist.

THE INTERPRETATION OF SHORT-RUN PRICE AND PROFIT TRENDS

One more important point needs to be made regarding market structure. We have argued vigorously throughout this study that because of the special characteristics of the land market, discussions of market power must be based on the potential supply of land and not on who in particular happens to develop land during a particular time period. It was argued that if developers have good expectations about the future, then a competitive equilibrium will tend to generate a time series of prices such that each developer (given identical rates of time preference, etc.) will be more or less indifferent to precisely when his land is developed. A competitive land market under these circumstances is quite consistent with a situation in which only one developer accounts for all sales of serviced lots in a given year.

This analysis abstracts from the fact that in any given year, the potential supply of serviced lots to the housing market is constrained to equal the number of lots approved for subdivision which have available servicing. We have noted that there are long lags between requesting subdivision approval and the granting of that approval. The result of this is that in any given year, the supply schedule for serviced lots is only elastic up to the point where supply equals the total number of undeveloped lots approved for subdivision. Beyond this point the supply becomes totally inelastic. During periods of time in which developers have correct expectations about future demands and supplies, an implication of the theory is that market equilibrium will not fall in the inelastic portion of supply in any one year. If such a situation did occur, it would imply that the owners of the lots in question were receiving a price higher than the price they would be willing to sell for, a situation inconsistent with competitive equilibrium under the assumptions noted.

The long lags involved in the subdivision approval process together with unforeseen fluctuations in demand, however, imply that in any particular year, the total number of lots that can actually be supplied to the market may fall far short of demand at what would be equilibrium prices if there were no lags in subdivision approvals. In such a situation, owners of land that is approved for subdivision and serviceable may be able to reap substantial *rents* but this is not, in itself, evidence of market power.

The point here is with demand uncertainty, the long lag time in subdivision approvals may generate short periods of high profits for a few lucky developers even in a competitive land market. This type of situation must not be confused with market power since optimal government policy is clearly different in the two cases. The problem of short-run disequilibrium in a competitive land market is best dealt with by ensuring that there is always a healthy stock of lots approved for subdivision which have readily available trunk servicing. Government policy is very important in determining the magnitude of fluctuations in lot prices arising from shocks to the land and housing markets.

SUMMARY AND CONCLUSIONS

(1) This chapter began with a brief critical discussion of previous statistical analyses of ownership concentration in the Toronto land market and proceeded to develop a methodology of ownership concentration analysis based on the theoretical findings of earlier chapters. The need to define properly the relevant universe of undeveloped land was emphasized and previous work was criticized

on this basis. It was also noted that the decision to sample only undeveloped land should result in a definite upward bias of our concentration statistics.

(2) Following a discussion of our sampling procedures, sample results were presented and analysed. The problems connected with defining effective ownership statistics were examined both for linking companies by overlaps in principal officers and directors and by overlaps in equity ownership. The former method was chosen for this study and effective ownership statistics were presented on this basis.

(3) The first result that emerged in both the nominal and in the effective ownership statistics was that concentration of ownership in the individual towns was much higher than the concentration over the entire sample area. Firms had a clear tendency to stick in one area and reasons why this might be a sound strategy were presented.

(4) A second result that occurred in both the nominal and effective ownership statistics both for the entire sample area and for the individual municipalities was that ownership concentration in the full sample was significantly lower than the concentration in the restricted sample (the full sample less land not likely to be developed in the next ten years). This suggested that land closer to development was more likely to be held by the larger companies and that land was traded up from small developers and speculators to larger developers as the time until development was approached. This conclusion is reinforced by the evidence presented in chapter 6. The implications of this conclusion will be discussed in detail in chapter 7.

(5) Under all sets of assumptions presented (full versus restricted sample and nominal versus effective ownership), ownership concentration in the entire sample area was far too low to suggest market power and resource misallocation under commonly used industrial organization standards. For several of the individual municipalities, effective ownership concentration in the restricted sample may be high enough to suggest the presence of market power, but only if consumers regarded land in different municipalities as very poor substitutes so that the individual municipalities define separate markets.

(6) It was also argued that barriers to effective collusion were very low in the land market since all transacted prices had to be registered by law. More to the point is the fact that an attempt by one firm to develop land in violation of a collusive agreement would be known several years ahead of actual development due to the delays in subdivision approval.

(7) The principal conclusion of this chapter, then, is that if households regard locations in different municipalities as very poor substitutes, then there may be a case for the existence market power in some regions of Toronto. If, however, lots in different municipalities are reasonably good substitutes, the case

for market power in the Toronto land market is very weak. In our opinion, since the individual municipalities do not form disjoint commuter sheds, it is the latter conclusion which is most likely to be valid.

(8) The implications of these findings are clear. The case for market power in the Toronto land market is quite weak, implying that the government must look elsewhere for explanations as to why prices rose to the high levels they did in 1973 and 1974. An alternate explanation based on (*a*) unanticipated increases in demand, (*b*) unanticipated shortages of trunk servicing capacity, and (*c*) unanticipated unwillingness of local municipalities to grant subdivision approvals at previous rates as discussed in the introduction to this study, emerges as a much stronger theory to explain these price surges. The different implications for public policy depending on whether this latter theory is correct or the monopoly control theory is correct are obvious. The monopoly theory puts the blame on developers while the unanticipated land shortage theory places the blame on the various levels of government. Both the theoretical and the empirical sections lend strong support to the conclusion that the unanticipated lot shortage theory is the correct one. Final analysis of this point and the recommendations deriving from it are left for the final section of this study.

6
Land assembly in
the Toronto region

INTRODUCTION

The previous chapter was concerned with a cross-section analysis of land ownership in the Toronto region and its principle conclusion was that concentration of
ownership was generally too low to imply significant market power. Given that
conclusion, we expect the qualitative behaviour of the land market to be roughly
as predicted in the competitive models outlined above. But the way in which the
qualitative results of those models translate into an actual time series of prices
and housing starts still depends on a number of parameters. Similarly, the
theoretical sections of this study have shown that the effects of government
intervention in the land market depend on a range of considerations in addition
to the existence or non-existence of market power.

The purpose of this chapter, therefore, is to arrive at an understanding of how
the land assembly and development process works in the Toronto area. This goal
embodies a number of empirical questions, the first of which is the question of
how long before subdivision do developers acquire land. If, as we will see, the
length of time is considerable, the long-run effects of the speculation tax (e.g.,
the effect of the tax on the land assembly process) may be slow in surfacing and
difficult to reverse. A second question that will be addressed is the extent to
which intermediary agents between farmer and developer are involved in the
process of assembling and holding land. The answer to this question has
important implications for the effects of government actions such as the Ontario
Land Speculation Tax. The frequency of sales among developers will also be of
interest here. A third set of empirical questions relate to the time span over

which land assembly takes place and the point in time at which prices begin to exceed agricultural opportunity costs. Answers to these questions help to quantify the supply response to short-run fluctuations. This information will also give us observations on how well the actual path of prices over time corresponds to theoretical results developed earlier.

A final set of empirical issues addressed below relate to the capital gains realized on land development and on the distribution of capital gains among original owners, intermediaries, and final developers. This question is particularly important in assessing how the Ontario Land Speculation Tax or other types of taxes (property tax, vacant land tax, etc.) can affect the development process. If most of the gains accrue to initial owners (farmers) and final developers, for example, the tax is likely to have less impact than if large capital gains are realized by intermediaries.[1]

SAMPLE DESIGN

The method chosen to realize the objectives set forth in the introduction to this chapter was to examine the history of land parcels (through registry records) which have been approved for subdivision or which were in the process of being approved. Primary data collection was again required on our part since we were unable to locate any studies which specifically addressed these issues. This was somewhat surprising (although we may have missed some existing data) in view of the long-standing public debate about developer land banking and its effect on land prices.

The problem faced with data collection of this type is simply that it is quite costly, and with limited resources, we were forced to restrict ourselves to a rather small sample. The ownership sample in the previous chapter was quite valuable in serving to identify land assemblies, and interviews with planners served to identify recent subdivision approvals and applications for approval. But given our significant sampling restrictions, a number of choices had to be made. First, should the sample concentrate on large or small subdivision areas? Statistics quoted from Muller (1976) in the previous chapter show that small subdivisions of less than 100 acres do account for a significant portion of all subdivision activity. On the other hand, his statistics also show that the top 10 developers accounted for about 60 per cent of the dwelling unit approvals during his sample period. A closely related problem was whether or not we should

1 The present structure of the Ontario Land Speculation Tax has a number of excape clauses which make it relatively easy for bona fide farmers and developers to avoid taxation. This will be discussed in greater detail in the next chapter.

concentrate on subdivisions of larger developers (whether or not the actual subdivisions were large or small) or attempt a relatively representative sampling procedure across all developers. While the latter is appealing, it would have left us with no more than two observations on any particular size of developer (or subdivision) if we were to form four size categories. Similarly, taking a random sample of something on the order of six to eight subdivisions did not seem to be an ideal procedure. Partly due to these concerns and partly due to the fact that public and political debate has focused on the role of the larger developers, our decision was to focus all our resources on large assemblies and subdivisions of the larger developers. Four such assemblies were then examined in detail as described below.

A final methodological problem we had to deal with concerned the time period within which we would conduct the study. We decided to devote all our efforts to examining the history of land parcels which were approved for subdivision in the early 1970's or for which application for subdivision approval was made in the same period. The disadvantages of this restriction and the restriction imposed in the previous section are obvious: what follows can claim to be representative only of relatively large land assemblies which arrived at the subdivision stage in the early 1970s. Therefore, for example, these assemblies cannot be assumed to be typical of the development process during the boom of the seventies. We would guess, however, that they are representitive of the workings of the development process during 'normal' times.

The advantages of these restrictions, on the other hand, are that we are left with a number of observations on roughly comparable events which gives us some basis for making general statements. Indeed, one of the principal conclusions which emerges from the data is that the four land assemblies examined have few patterns in common. Such a conclusion could hardly be drawn from a sample which had only one observation each on a number of non-comparable (in size or time) assemblies or subdivisions.

The first (in arbitrary order) assembly chosen for study was owned by Monarch Construction. The location is Markham, Concession 6, Lots 13-15. A rough outline of the assembly is shown in Figure 6 and the assembly process is shown in Figure 7.[2] The second assembly, shown in Figures 8 and 9, owned by

---

2 All municipalities in this region are divided into strips which are called concessions. Each concession strip is then divided into a number of lots. While the width of concessions and the shape of lots varies among the municipalities, all lots are 200 acres in area. In Figure 6, for example, the concession runs north-south and Lot 13, composed of parcels number 1 and 2, measures 0.25 x 1.25 miles. Parcels 3 and 4 are the west halves of Lots 14 and 15 respectively and are each approximately 100 acres in area. In the tables corresponding to the figures, the left-hand column lists the parcel numbers found on the

Markborough, is located in Mississauga, Concession 6, Lots 7-11. The third assembly is in Brampton, Concession 3, Lots 7-10 which is part of Bramalea Consolidated's large holdings in the area and is shown in Figures 10 and 11. The final assembly is owned by Cadillac-Fairview and is located in Mississauga, Concession 6, Lots 1-5. This assembly is shown in Figures 12 and 13. Each of these diagrams is a stylized representation of the actual process. The actual processes, details of which were obtained from registry records in the respective towns, are much more lengthy histories of grants, deeds, quit claims, and agreements for sale. These histories are characterized by a large number of minor severances, easements by owners to municipalities or utility companies, etc. A completely accurate history of the Cadillac assembly in Mississauga, for example, would require well in excess of 100 pieces of information in addition to those presented in Figure 13. What we have done, therefore, is to reduce the mass of information obtained from the registry records to that set of information that reveals clearly the structure of the assembly process. It is sufficient to note here that in a number of cases there have been *minor* changes in the various land parcels as they move through time, owing to such things as easements to municipalities. Boundary lines in Figures 6, 8, 10, and 12 are also stylized and should not be taken literally.

Before proceeding to analyse the data, some comments on sales prices and the implied capital gains in Figures 7, 9, 11, and 13 are in order. We wish to emphasize that the gross capital gains implied by these figures are gains associated *only* with successful development efforts. Under no circumstances should these figures be taken as representative of the average capital gains earned on land in the ownership sample presented in the previous chapter. In fact, it is quite reasonable to suppose that the capital gains made on some of the land in this sample are among the very highest gains realized anywhere in the Toronto region during this period. Estimating capital gains from land speculation is not an objective of this study and the sales prices given below cannot be used for such purposes.[3] If asked to adopt a position, we would guess that the rates of

---

figures. The first name listed is a seller and the second name is a buyer with the date of the transaction given below the names. Acreage figures and sale prices (unless not available (NA)) are also given. The transacting parties are under penalty of law to report the correct sale price since there is a small *ad valorem* transfer tax. However, the tax can be paid directly to the tax authorities rather than to the registry which explains why, in some cases, the sale price does not appear in registry records.

3 Recalling our discussion in chapter 4, in order to quantify meaningfully 'average' capital gains on land speculation, the differential 'riskiness' of land would have to be controlled for.

capital gains given below overstate average capital gains by several orders of magnitude during the time period under consideration.

In addition to asserting that the capital gains reported below are by no means representative, we must point out that no attempt is made to impute these gains to productive versus speculative sources. Some of the gains can likely be imputed to productive functions such as zoning changes, roads, and other improvements, value added by assembling a parcel sufficiently large for profitable subdivision, and so forth. We have made no attempt to separate out value added owing to these changes. Similarly, in the case of risky investments some capital gains must be imputed to the investor's willingness to bear risk. Buying unzoned agricultural land above agricultural opportunity cost is very definitely a risky investment. As discussed below, the fact that in the particular cases treated here certain speculative agents made large capital gains does not necessarily imply that the speculator had better information or otherwise 'cheated' the farmer out of his land; it may only imply that the speculator was willing to bear more risk or had a lower rate of time preference.

Finally, the recorded date of transactions may be misleading, since many of the transactions may represent the exercise of *options*, on which we have no information.

MONARCH CONSTRUCTION ASSEMBLY IN MARKHAM

The first assembly that we will consider is land held by Monarch Construction in the town of Markham (see Figure 5). This land area is depicted in Figure 6 and the assembly process is shown in Figure 7. The first characteristic we can note from Figure 7 is that the individual land holdings in this assembly are relatively large, the assembly being composed of four parcels of 106, 95, 102, and 103 acres for a total acreage of 405. The advantage to a development company of assembling a fixed acreage from relatively large holdings is obviously that the number of transactions are minimized.

The left hand column of Figure 7 gives an initial set of transactions on this land with the transactions of parcels 3 and 4 giving some idea of the value of this land in the early 1950s. It must be emphasized that we have no way of knowing what structures, such as houses or barns, were on these parcels and hence have no way of separating the land component of the sale price from the total. In any case, parcel 3 was sold in 1952 for $50,000 which comes to about $490 per acre while parcel 4 was sold in 1951 for $35,000 which is about $340 per acre. These sale prices are not out of line with the agricultural value of land during this period especially if the two parcels did have houses or farm buildings on them. It would seem, then, that we can advance the proposition that as of 1951-2, the market

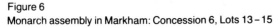

Figure 6
Monarch assembly in Markham: Concession 6, Lots 13 – 15

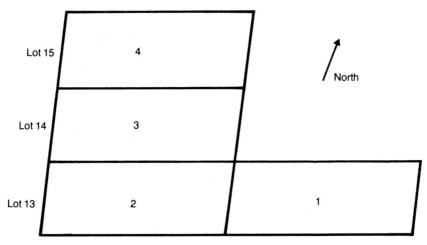

did not perceive the increase in land values in this area that would occur in the next thirty years. This is not very surprising, since in the early fifties there was considerable uncertainty about the future growth rate of Toronto, and about direction of future expansion.

The next set of transactions occurred between September 1965 and January 1968 as shown in Figure 7. During this period, all of the land in question was sold by private individuals to Realty or Development Companies. The three companies involved, Crosley Realty, Uniongate Developments, and Simon-Henry Ltd. are independent companies to the best of our knowledge. Sale prices on these three transactions ranged from $1990 per acre on the McKay to Crosley transaction to $2489 per acre on the Gardhouse to Uniongate sale. Such prices far exceed agricultural opportunity costs and clearly reflect expectations of development potential. (Notice however that Buchanan (parcel 4), for example, made a *gross* annual rate-of-return of only slightly more than 7 per cent.) To the best of our knowledge, none of the companies involved actually engage in any sort of development activities, and can probably be labelled speculators under the definition adopted in this study.

The three parcels were subsequently consolidated into one in the six months period between December 1968 and May 1969 during which all three were sold to Schikedanz. Sale prices ranged from $4725 per acre on the Simon-Henry to

Figure 7
Monarch assembly in Markham

1	Gormley – McKay 29 May 1933	106 ac NA	McKay – Crosley Realty 29 September 1965	201 ac $400,000	Crosley – Schikedanz 22 April 1969	201 ac $1,110,824	Schikedanz – Monarch 15 April 1969	405 ac $3,247,400
2	Gormley – McKay 20 October 1932	95 ac NA					
3	Savage – Gardhouse 29 July 1952	102 ac $50,000	Gardhouse – Uniongate 1 December 1966	102 ac $253,890	Uniongate – Schikedanz 16 May 1969	102 ac $558,558	
4	Hambly – Buchanan 14 November 1951	103 ac $35,000	Buchanan – Simon Henry 31 January 1968	103 ac $236,600	Simon Henry – Schikedanz 10 December 1968	103 ac $486,675	

Schikedanz transaction to $5526 per acre on the Crosley-Schikedanz trans-action. In each case, the *gross* annual rate-of-return realized by the speculative agents exceeded 30 per cent. Schikedanz, unlike the other companies involved, is a company which engages in development and construction activities. It is not clear, therefore, what the company's initial intentions were in making these purchases. What is clear is that even before one Schikedanz transaction had been registered (the Uniongate-Schikedanz sale), Schikedanz sold the whole assembly to Monarch Construction for $3,247,000 in April 1969. This sale price of $8058 per acre represented a gross capital gain of $1,091,343 in a very short period of time, over the total purchase price of $2,156,057 paid for the three parcels.

The degree of capital gains made at the various stages of this land assembly could possibly be explained in a number of ways. The first is the increase in value due to assembling land. Schikedanz did perform a useful economic function in assembling the three separate parcels. However the return realized by Schikedanz seems too large to be fully explained by this. Part of the gains made by the speculative intermediaries could have been due to better information or more accurate expectations on their part relative to the individuals from whom they purchased the land. On the other hand, it must be emphasized again that the purchases made by these intermediaries were risky and it is completely possible that the gains made by these companies are simply outlyers in the distribution of returns to risk bearing. The gains realized by Schikedanz, how-ever, are harder to explain by risk bearing and likely signal the existence of imperfect information. Why the three speculative companies could not deal directly with Monarch is hard to understand. However, Schikedanz may have held options on the three parcels. It may not be unreasonable to impute the gains made by Schikedanz as rents due to superior information and not to returns to risk bearing.

Briefly summing up, this Monarch assembly was made up by the amalgama-tion of a small number of relatively large parcels. There is no evidence that the future value of the land was perceived by the market 18 years prior to its purchase by Monarch, during which time the price per acre of the land appre-ciated by a factor in excess of 16 (a *gross* annual rate of 18 per cent). Land holding during this 18-year period did involve a set of speculative agents who sold the land to one developer who turned the land over to the final owner for a substantial capital gain.

MARKBOROUGH ASSEMBLY IN MISSISSAUGA

The second assembly we will look at is land held by Markborough in the City of Mississauga. This land is part of Markborough's Meadowvale development and is depicted in Figure 8. The assembly process is given in Figure 9. The individual land parcels making up this assembly are again of reasonably large size, the smallest original holding being the 98 acres of parcels 10 and 11.

The left hand column of Figure 9 reveals that the pattern of land assembly here is quite different from the Monarch assembly discussed in the previous section. In the present case, Erin Mills development company assembled an entire 825 acres (parcels 2 through 11 in Figure 8) in the space of six months from May 1956 to November 1956. Some indication about the tremendous degree of price appreciation, however, can be gained from transactions in the late 1940s on parcels 2, 10, and 11. Parcel 2 was sold by a party named Christiansen to a party named Colpitis in November 1949 for $14,000, which amounts to only $133 per acre for the 105 acres. Parcels 10 and 11 were sold by a party named Cantilon to a party named Nixon in May 1948 for $6800 which comes to $77 per acre for the 87 acres involved. These figures do not exceed agricultural value and thereby suggest that the market did not anticipate the degree of price appreciation that was to follow.

In May 1956, Erin Mills developments made its first purchases. A party named McIntyre sold parcel 3 for $101,721 which came to $997 per acre for the 102 acres. A party named Leslie sold parcels 4 and 5 for $78,305 which amounted to $522 per acre for the 150 acres. Finally, a party named Sparling sold parcel 9 for $83,452 which came to $499 per acre for the 167 acres involved. Later, in September of 1956, parcels 6, 7, and 8 were sold by Weylie to Erin Mills for $218,675 or $1375 per acre for the 159 acres. The final piece was acquired from Nixon (parcels 10 and 11) at $186,649 or $2,121 per acre in November of 1956.

This assembly of 825 acres (parcels 2 through 11) by Erin Mills is characterized by several features: first, the short length of time in which it was assembled; second, the wide variation in the prices paid per acre for the land. These prices ranged from $499 per acre for parcel 9 to $2121 per acre for parcels 10 and 11. It seems unlikely to us that these differences could have been entirely due to the presence of houses or farm buildings on the higher priced land and we know of no particular locational or topographical advantage enjoyed by the higher priced land. As a matter of fact, in the case of the highest priced land (parcels 10 and 11) it appears that a house and lot were severed from the parcel when it was originally transferred from Cantilon to Nixon, suggesting that there was no house on these lots to add to the sale price. This result again suggests that there was imperfect information in the market and, in particular, that each landowner (or at least some landowners) was not aware of what Erin Mills was offering the other landowners. This suspicion is reinforced by another distinguishing feature of this assembly. Note that land parcels sold later in the year

Figure 8
Markborough assembly in Mississauga:
Concession 6, Lots 7 – 11

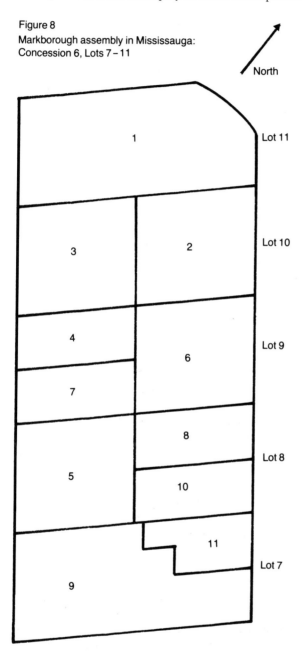

Figure 9
Markborough assembly in Mississauga

#					
1		Waite – Magee 13 August 1957 — 192 ac $192,096		Magee – Markborough 5 November 1969 — 192 ac $1,920,960	
2	Christinsen – Colpitis 11 November 1949 — 105 ac $14,000	Colpitis – Erin Mills 29 August 1956 — 105 ac NA	Erin Mills – Don Mills 10 January 1966 — 825 ac NA	Don Mills – Markborough 11 November 1971* — 826 ac $2,482,711	
3		McIntyre – Erin Mills 17 May 1956 — 102 ac $101,721			
4		Leslie – Erin Mills 17 May 1956 — 50 ac			
5		Leslie – Erin Mills 17 May 1956 — 100 ac $78,305			
6		Weylie – Erin Mills 20 September 1956 — 104 ac			
7		Weylie – Erin Mills 20 September 1956 — 53 ac			
8		Weylie – Erin Mills 20 September 1956 — 52 ac $218,675			
9		Sparling – Erin Mills 22 May 1956 — 167 ac $83,452			
10	Cantilon – Nixon 26 May 1948 — 47 ac	Nixon – Erin Mills 18 November 1956 — 88 ac $186,649			
11	Cantilon – Nixon 26 May 1948 — 41 ac $6,800				

* This date represents the closing of an agreement for sale contracted in 1957 between Erin Mills and Markborough.

commanded increasingly higher prices per acre. Land sold by Weylie in September brought an average of $1375 per acre while the land sold by Nixon in November went for $2121 per acre. Both figures are significantly higher than the prices paid for land the previous May. Assuming that Erin Mills made offers to Weylie and Nixon at the same time as offers were made to the other land owners, the former played a successful strategy in holding out for the short period of several months. Of course, if all owners had held out for $2000 per acre, Erin Mills may have scrapped the site altogether. In any case, the average price paid by Erin Mills was $929 per acre, so presumably the company would have been willing to pay at least this much had it been offered the entire parcel by a single owner. Such reasoning leads directly to the conclusion that the owners who sold for less did not have good information.

Figure 9 next shows that the lands acquired by Erin Mills were transferred to Don Mills Developments in January 1966. This was a paper transaction only, since the founders and principal officers of Erin Mills (privately held by those individuals) are also officers and apparently equity owners of Don Mills. Don Mills, in turn, was amalgamated into Cadillac-Fairview in May 1974. As far as we know, Don Mills was an actual development company and not just a speculative holding company. Nevertheless, the company chose to sell its holdings to Markborough in November of 1971 as shown in Figure 9. The sale price of this transaction was $2,482,711. This 1971 date actually represents the closing date of an agreement for sale contracted in 1957, which explains the low sale price. To be consistent, we have reported dates of deed transfers throughout this chapter, an approach that has disadvantages in a case such as this.

An additional section added to Markborough's holdings in this Concession was parcel 1 shown in Figure 8. This parcel was sold by a party named Waite to Elaine S. Magee in 1957 for $192,096 or $1000 per acre. This appears to have been a speculative purchase and was held by Magee until 1969 at which time it was sold to Markborough for $1,920,960 or $10,000 per acre (a *gross* annual rate-of-return of about 21 per cent) as shown in Figure 9.

Summing up, the Markborough holdings in Concession 6 west in Mississauga were primarily assembled by Erin Mills Developments in the short span of six months in 1969. No other speculative agents (with the possible exception of Nixon and Colpitis) appear to have been involved. The assembly is characterized by large differences in the prices paid per acre with those who sold later receiving higher prices per acre. One additional purchase was made by Markborough from a private party who realized substantial capital gains on what appears to be a speculative purchase.

BRAMALEA ASSEMBLY IN BRAMPTON

The third assembly we shall consider is one section of Bramalea Consolidated's substantial holdings in the City of Brampton. This section is located in Concession 3 east, lots 7-10 which is to the northeast of the Brampton business district. The structure of the assembly is shown in Figure 10 and the assembly process is shown in Figure 11. As in the previous cases, the individual plots comprising the assembly are of reasonably large size as shown in the left hand column of Figure 11.

Most of the transactions on this land in the 1940s and in the early 1950's were between members of the same family and do not give useful price information. There are two exceptions, however, the first of which was the sale of parcel 1 by a party named Moran to a party named Ruston in July 1951. The sale price was $5000 or only $100 per acre. The second transaction was the sale of parcel 3 by the same Moran to a party named Clarkson in April 1953. The recorded price was $26,000 or about $286 per acre. Both prices were within the upper limit of possible agricultural value, suggesting that the market did not anticipate the increase in land values that was to follow. These figures are notably lower than the two transactions which occurred during this period on the Monarch lands in Markham.

The second series of transactions which took place all involved sales by private individuals to holding companies. Ruston sold parcels 1 and 2 to Bayton Holdings in December 1957 for $166,216 or about $1108 per acre. Clarkson sold parcel 3 to Arosa Properties for $631,936 or approximately $6,514 per acre fifteen years later in 1972. Parcel 4 was sold by J. Ackroyd in October 1955 to Nortonville Holdings for $150,000 or $5,000 per acre. Finally, M. Ackroyd sold parcel 7 to Armstrong Brothers in March 1964 for $138,614 or about $2,718 per acre. Since these transactions occurred on widely separated dates, we cannot make the same sort of cross-section comparison of sale prices that we made in connection with the Markborough lands. Note, however, that the sale prices per acre increase over time with the exception of the unusual J. Ackroyd-Nortonville sale, which resulted in a substantial loss for Nortonville Holdings as shown in the next column. All of these four purchases seem to have been speculative in nature. In particular, Bayton Holdings, Arosa Properties, and Nortonville Holdings never did and do not now engage in any actual development activities to the best of our knowledge. Note also that the data once again point to the mid 1950s as the date at which land prices began significantly to exceed agricultural value. In the present case, this is documented by the Ruston to Bayton sale for $1108 per acre. This follows the same pattern found in the Monarch and

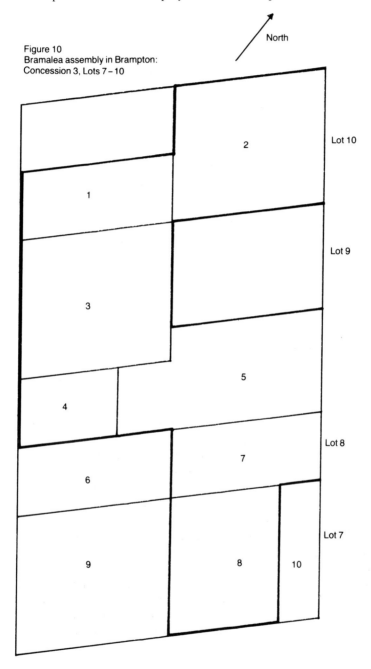

Figure 10
Bramalea assembly in Brampton:
Concession 3, Lots 7–10

Figure 11
Bramalea assembly in Brampton

#	Transaction	ac / $	Transaction	ac / $	Transaction	ac / $
1	Moran – Ruston 15 July 1951	50 ac $5,000	Ruston – Bayton 16 December 1957	150 ac $166,216	Bayton – Bramalea 28 March 1958	150 ac NA
2	Ruston – Ruston 10 January 1948	100 ac Nil				
3	Moran – Clarkson 1 April 1953	97 ac $26,000	Clarkson – Arosa 10 August 1972	97 ac $631,936	Arosa – Bramalea 16 March 1973	97 ac $1,323,469
4	Ackroyd – J. Ackroyd 14 December 1942	30 ac	J. Ackroyd – Nortonville 1 October 1955	30 ac $150,000	Nortonville – Bramalea 15 November 1963	30 ac $75,000
5	Ackroyd – J. Ackroyd 14 December 1942	97 ac $4,500			J. Ackroyd – Bramalea 15 November 1963	97 ac $243,145
6	Ackroyd – M. Ackroyd 21 May 1943	49 ac				
7	Ackroyd – M. Ackroyd 21 May 1943	51 ac $3,000	M. Ackroyd – Armstrong 16 March 1964	51 ac $138,614	Armstrong – Bramalea 27 April 1964	51 ac $141,243
8	Parr – M. Parr 17 April 1943	72 ac			M. Parr – Bramalea 31 March 1970	72 ac $1,149,760
9	Parr – M. Parr 17 April 1943	100 ac				
10	Parr – M. Parr 17 April 1943	26 ac $19,500				

Markborough assemblies: prices did not exceed agricultural value in the early 1950s but by the mid 1950s, prices were significantly in excess of this value.

The final set of transactions involved the sale of the individual parcels to Bramalea Consolidated. The difference between this assembly and the previous two assemblies examined lies in the fact that acquisition of the land by the final user was spread over a fairly long period of time. The first piece was obtained from Bayton Holdings in March 1958 (sale price was not recorded on the registry instrument). The second purchase was parcel 4 from Nortonville in November 1963 for $75,000 or $2500 per acre. Parcel 7 was then acquired from Armstrong Brothers for $141,243 or about $2769 per acre. The fourth purchase was parcel 8 which was acquired from a private individual, M. Parr, for $1,149,760 or about $15,969 per acre in March 1970. Arosa Properties sold parcel 3 in May 1970 for $1,323,469 or about $13,644 per acre in May 1973. Finally, J. Ackroyd sold parcel 5 in November 1963 for $243,145 or a much lower figure of $2506 per acre. The lands were, therefore, assembled by Bramalea over a period of 15 years. This stands in sharp contrast to the Markborough assembly which was put together by Erin Mills Developments in the short space of six months and the Monarch assembly which was put together by Schikedanz in five months. The Bramalea assembly also stands in contrast to the other two in that it was the final user who put the assembly together, which was not true in the other two cases.

Large capital gains can be found in this assembly but the variance of the possible returns to speculation is also strikingly evident. While Arosa Properties made a gross capital gain of $691,533 in nine months, Nortonville Holdings had a gross capital loss of $75,000 in its venture. The actual loss to Nortonville was well over $100,000 when taxes and foregone interest are considered.[4] Between these two extremes was the Armstrong transaction which netted a gross profit of $2629. While positive, it is unlikely that this figure netted a profit after taxes and transactions costs. Thus while gross rates-of-return on the aggregate of these three properties was large the variance illustrates the risks involved in land speculation. This, in turn, illustrates why it is perfectly rational for an individual like J. Ackroyd to sell out to an intermediary like Nortonville Holdings and shows why incidences of high capital gains made by speculators do not necessarily imply that a poor farmer was duped.

---

4 Compounding $150,000 for eight years even at 5 per cent brings the investment to $221,618. Subtracting the $75,000 sale price then leaves a loss of $146,618. This of course neglects taxes and other costs.

CADILLAC-FAIRVIEW ASSEMBLY IN MISSISSAUGA

The final land assembly we will examine is a section of the Cadillac-Fairview Corporation holdings in Mississauga. This land is located at the southwestern edge of Mississauga, Concession 6, Lots 1-5 and lies to the southeast of the Markborough lands discussed earlier. This area is depicted in Figure 12 and the assembly process is shown in Figure 13. This land is more fragmented than the other lands we have dealt with, having parcels under 15 acres.

The first two columns of Table 6.4 reveal a process that is the same as that examined in the previous three assemblies. A striking feature is again that land prices did not begin to rise above agricultural value until well into 1955. Parcel 3 was transacted from a party named Cook to a party named Galagher in October 1951 for $2000 or $400 per acre. Rutledge fragmented his holdings into four pieces, retaining one piece and selling three pieces off between 1949 and 1953. This is the only example of land fragmentation in the four assemblies. Parcel 17, sold by Rutledge to Zimonczyk in December 1952, brought $300 per acre. Parcel 16, which Rutledge sold to Petersen in April 1953 went for only $239 per acre. Zimonczyk held parcel 17 only until May 1955 at which time it was sold to a party named Prentice for $15,000 or $1500 per acre (which represents a *gross* annual rate-of-return of about 90 per cent). This fivefold appreciation in the value of parcel 17 is a signal that somewhere in early 1955 the coming increase in values was perceived.

Erin Mills Developments began the assembly with a purchase of parcel 8 from Louise Bonham for $517 per acre. Subsequent purchases through June 1956 brought from a low of $497 per acre (parcel 13) to a high of $7000 per acre (parcel 3). The other small parcels in addition to parcel 3 sold for substantially higher prices per acre than the larger parcels which perhaps reflects the price of houses averaged over all the acreage. In any case, the assembly was completed (with the exception of parcels 7 and 11 to be acquired later by Don Mills) in October 1959 with the purchase of parcel 16 for $2889 per acre. It is interesting to note that although Pearson did not sell for an additional 3 years, the price he received was about the same as the 1956 prices per acre received for similar size pieces such as parcel 15 ($2844 per acre), parcel 17 ($3036), and parcel 9 ($4250).

On 31 December 1965, Erin Mills transferred the titles to Don Mills Developments which subsequently merged with Cadillac-Fairview. As noted earlier, this was a change in name only and involved no monetary payment. Two final parcels were added under the Don Mills name, the first being parcel 7 in May 1967 for $2528 per acre and the second being parcel 11 in January 1969 for $17,500 per acre (likely reflecting a house on the land).

Figure 12
Cadillac assembly in Mississauga:
Concession 6, Lots 1–5

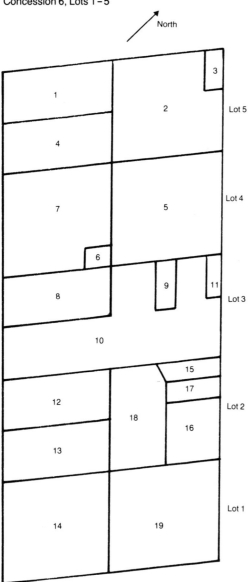

Figure 13
Cadillac assembly in Mississauga

#	Transaction 1	Transaction 2	Transaction 3	Erin Mills / Don Mills acquisition	Final transfer
1	Cook – Cook 25 November 1889 · 52 ac NA			Cook – Erin Mills 4 May 1956 · 147 ac $90,270	Erin Mills – Don Mills 31 December 1956 · 308 ac NA
2	Turvey – Cook 15 June 1945 · 95 ac				
3	Turvey – Cook 15 June 1945 · 5 ac $2,500	Cook – Galagher 2 October 1951 · 5 ac $2,000		Galagher – Erin Mills 13 January 1956 · 5 ac $35,000	
4	Carter – Prince 1 December 1948 · 151 ac $11,500			Prince – Erin Mills 12 May 1956 · 151 ac $107,460	
5					
6	Gerrie – Wigley 6 June 1941 · 5 ac $2,000			Wigley – Erin Mills 24 April 1964 · 5 ac $25,000	
7	Richie – Natwary 15 May 1943 · 95 ac $5,500			Natwary – Don Mills 25 May 1967 · 95 ac $240,167	
8	Bonham – L. Bonham 22 March 1951 · 50 ac Nil			L. Bonham – Erin Mills 20 October 1955 · 50 ac $25,857	Lands retained by Erin Mills
9	Bonham – Armstrong 20 September 1950 · 10 ac $4,750			Armstrong – Erin Mills 5 January 1956 · 10 ac $42,500	
10	Bonham – Karl 7 December 1945 · 144 ac $11,500			Karl – Erin Mills 25 May 1956 · 140 ac $83,916	
11					Karl – Don Mills 13 January 1969 · 4 ac $70,000
12	McCracken – McCracken 27 April 1945 · 50 ac $2,800			McCracken – Erin Mills 21 August 1956 · 50 ac $45,080	Erin Mills – Don Mills 31 December 1965 · 400 ac NA
13	Onyschuk – Strandholt 31 May 1950 · 50 ac $8,000			Strandholt – Erin Mills 25 May 1956 · 50 ac $24,845	
14	McLeod – Stephens 7 December 1939 · 100 ac $6,500			Stephens – Erin Mills 22 June 1956 · 100 ac $78,867	
15	Donaldson – C. Rutledge 1 July 1949 · 100 ac $6,500	C. Rutledge – Ronowski 20 September 1949 · 14 ac $3,800		Ronowski – Erin Mills 19 October 1956 · 14 ac $39,827	
16		C. Rutledge – Peterson 1 April 1953 · 23 ac $5,500		Peterson – Erin Mills 19 October 1959 · 23 ac $66,442	
17		C. Rutledge – Zimonczyk 12 December 952 · 10 ac $3,000	Zimonczyk – Prentice 9 May 1955 · 10 ac $15,000	Prentice – Erin Mills 10 January 1956 · 10 ac $30,363	
18				C. Rutledge – Erin Mills 25 May 1956 · 153 ac $111,303	
19	Stewart – Rutledge 1 April 1926 · 100 ac $7,900				

It is no doubt evident to the reader that this assembly by Erin Mills Developments was carried on simultaneously with and adjacent to the Erin Mills assembly that was subsequently sold to Markborough (see the fourth section of this chapter). Indeed, there is no reason that we should not consider both assemblies simply as one, that was later split between the assembling company and a second company (we had no *a priori* knowledge that both were assembled by Erin Mills). Comments concerning the assembly process, degree of capital gains, distribution of capital gains, etc. in connection with the Markborough assembly, therefore, apply equally well here and will not be repeated, with one exception. This Erin Mills-Don Mills-Cadillac assembly took place without any intermediaries. No speculative land holding companies ever owned an acre of this land. Cadillac-Fairview Corporation itself began developing the land in the early 1970s about 18 years after its assembly. A good deal of the actual housing construction is being done by Cadillac's own building division. In this respect, the Cadillac assembly presents an interesting contrast to the other three assemblies in each of which some companies other than the final developer were involved.

SUMMARY AND CONCLUSIONS

(1) This chapter examined the histories of four land assemblies that were either subdivided in the early 1970s or for which subdivision approval was applied for during the same period. In each case, registry records of transactions showed that in the early 1950s land prices did not exceed agricultural value and, therefore, that the market did not perceive the tremendous price appreciation that would follow. This is certainly not surprising, given the uncertainty at the time about the future growth rate and direction of expansion of Toronto. In every case, prices first exceeded agricultural value between 1955 and 1956 or about twenty years before actual development was to take place. Prices continued to appreciate from the mid-1950s until the present, with prices in the early 1970s being as much as forty to fifty times the prices recorded in the early 1950s. This pattern, which was observed in each of the assemblies, is consistent with the theory presented earlier in chapter 3. That chapter and the subsequent chapter predicted that land prices should stay constant at agricultural value until demand (present and future) pushed prices above that value. Once above agricultural value, it was predicted that prices would appreciate continuously until the land was developed. If there is any consistency at all between the observed price paths and the paths predicted in the theory, it is that the rates of price appreciation were steeper than we would have predicted. Nevertheless, the actual pattern of prices is consistent with the theory if the degree of uncertainty in the land market was quite high, which seems a very reasonable assumption.

(2) In three of four assemblies (all except the Cadillac land), there were intermediary speculative agents between the farmer and the final developer. In at least two of the cases (Monarch and Bramalea), it appears that the intermediaries were speculators who did not engage in any actual development activities. Other intermediaries in the cases of the Monarch and Markborough assemblies were actual development companies, indicating that sales of undeveloped land among developers is not uncommon.

(3) Prices paid to private owners by speculative agents and final developers showed a high degree of variance. While some of this variance can be explained by the existence of structures on some parcels or special locational advantages, it is our opinion that such factors cannot entirely explain this variance. We suggest that some of the variance is probably due to imperfect information in the market. (Some of the variance is likely due to differential risk aversion and time preferences.) If we assume that, on the average, speculative companies and developers had better information than the private owners, the existence of imperfect information probably resulted in a transfer of capital gains from the farmers to the speculators and the developers relative to a perfect information situation.

(4) Average *gross* rates-of-return made by the intermediary agents were substantial and in some cases were spectacular. Yet the risk in this type of investment was illustrated in the Bramalea assembly where one speculator lost in excess of $100,000. We also emphasize, once again that there is an extreme bias in this sample toward high capital gains since we are only looking at land assemblies which did attract large developers and which have been or will be successfully developed. These capital gains must not be taken as representative of gains made on the average land in our ownership sample and the low incidence of losses must not be taken as evidence of low risk. It is also emphasized that high capital gains made by speculators are not in themselves evidence that speculators had better information or otherwise duped the farmers. Such gains may only indicate a willingness to bear risk and a willingness to wait twenty years before realizing a return on their investment. Nevertheless, the data do suggest that there was some degree of imperfect information in the market and, therefore, that some portion of the capital gains made by the speculators was a return to better information (*not* a return to market power. On this point see chapter 4).

(5) The time period over which land ownership was consolidated differed among the four assemblies. The Bramalea assembly was put together over a period of 15 years. In the other three cases, however, most of the land was consolidated by one agent within a few months. In the Monarch case, it was entirely done within six months, although it should be noted that this assembly was composed of only four parcels. Similarly, the time lag between assembly completion and subdivision application, what agent (intermediary or final

developer) was responsible for assembly, and the lag between the time the final developer acquired the land and the time subdivision approval was applied for all varied widely among the four assemblies. No general pattern seemed to emerge in any of these respects. The empirical results of this chapter and the preceding chapter, therefore, seem to be quite consistent with the theory developed in Chapters 3 and 4 under the assumptions that (*a*) the land market is competitive, and (*b*) there is a high degree of uncertainty. The reader should note that the land assemblies which we have described all took place before the speculative boom of the seventies. Therefore these assemblies cannot be taken to be representative of the development process during the seventies. We would guess however that they are representative of the development process during 'normal' times.

7
Implications for public policy

The first theoretical problem we dealt with was the connection between concentration of land ownership and the existence of potential market power in the land market. Unlike most markets, we showed that concentration is, itself, a sufficient condition for the existence of potential market power. We argued that the appropriate basis of the measure of concentration for a suitably defined urban area is the totality of 'developable' and developed (residential) land within the estimated future boundaries of the urban area. The existence of 'significant' concentration at the outer boundaries of development was shown to be a sufficient condition for the existence of exercised market power. It was argued that the (price) elasticity of demand for land determines what levels of concentration are 'significant' in a particular context.

These findings were then applied to an empirical study of ownership concentration in the Toronto region. A sample was designed using land that was within 30 to 45 minutes commuting distance from major Toronto employment centres. The inner figure is approximately the present outer boundary of heavily built up areas. Land which could not be serviced within the next ten years was eliminated from the sample as was all land in holdings under two acres or land held as industrial or commercial property. Ownership was determined for this sample of land and results clearly showed that ownership concentration in the entire region was far too low to imply market power, even when land judged unlikely to be developed in the next ten years was eliminated. Concentration in the individual municipalities around Toronto was significantly higher, and it was argued that a case for the existence of market power might be made if the different municipalities (or smaller sub-areas) could be considered to be separate markets. This could be possible if consumers regarded land in different municipalities to be very poor substitutes (i.e., cross elasticities of demand for land at different locations are low). However, we do not regard this as a reasonable possibility. For example, none of the municipalities forms a disjoint commuter shed, which indicates that employment location does not, in itself, suggest that the different municipalities should be considered to be separate markets. For the Toronto land market to differ from competition, there must be significant concentration either in the ownership of land or in the production of serviced land. This study argues that there is not significant concentration of land ownership in the Toronto area. Muller (1976) shows that there is not significant concentration in the production of serviced land.

We next constructed a general equilibrium, perfect foresight model of the land market, which we argued was a reasonable approximation of a land market in long-run equilibrium. Our analysis dealt with the timing of land development under competitive versus monopolistic market conditions, the rate of price appreciation under each market structure, and the effects of taxation. The analysis showed that land prices would remain at agricultural value until present and future market demand bid prices rise above that level. Once in excess of agricultural value, prices under competition would tend to appreciate continually at a rate which will approach the land investor's discount rate. The equilibrium path of prices under monopoly, on the other hand, depends upon a number of demand elasticities so that equilibrium prices may either rise or fall over time. We showed that the monopolist cannot both slow the rate of development and increase the rate of price appreciation.

The effects of two different types of taxes were analysed. A tax on land value appreciation will tend to increase the equilibrium rate of price appreciation and increase the rate of development in a competitive situation. The effects of the tax in a monopoly situation are unclear since they depend upon the same elasticities mentioned above. A property tax will lower the level of prices and increase the rate of price appreciation but its effect on the rate of development is unclear in the competitive situation. The effects of the property tax under monopoly are once again indeterminate.

Finally, the effects of uncertainty and speculation on the functioning of the land market were analysed. We argued that land is not homogeneous with respect to risk, and so the rate of return to speculation will be different for different types of land, and these rates of return will be related to each other and to rates of return on other assets. We constructed a general equilibrium model of the land market which had markets for developed and underdeveloped land, and where agents were uncertain about future prices and developers were also uncertain about the subdivision approval process. We showed that the existence of uncertainty and agents with better information than others does *not* imply the existence of market power. Thus, in the absence of concentrated ownership, the land market will be competitive, but the lack of a well-co-ordinated, centralized market and imperfect information flows result in the market operating less efficiently than more well-organized markets. It was shown that expectations about future prices and the approval process and the expecta-tions-forming mechanism can have significant effects on price and the rate of development in the short run. Therefore incorrect expectations can greatly impair the efficiency of allocation in the short run. We argued that the real estate boom in the Toronto area during the seventies was the result of the combination of an unforeseen increase in demand (an increase in the asset demand for land due to the enactment of capital gains taxation and the period of increasing inflation) and a shortage of serviced, approved land.

In a second empirical exercise we traced the histories of four Toronto land assemblies that are now at or near the sub-division stage. These four assemblies revealed a number of interesting facts which helped to quantify some of the aspects of our theoretical analysis. First, in each case prices first began to exceed agricultural value about 20 years before development. Prices generally continued to appreciate at high rates up to the time the final developer acquired the land. Second, in three of the four assemblies there were intermediary speculative agents between the farmer and the final developer. Prices paid to farmers by these intermediary agents showed a high degree of variance, suggesting the presence of significant uncertainty in the market. Third, while the average capital gains made by the speculators were very high, the risk present was illustrated by one large loss. It was also emphasized that this sample probably greatly overstates the average capital gains made on land speculation during this period since we were dealing only with successful land assemblies (i.e., land which is going to be developed by a large developer). Finally, it was shown that there were no particular patterns in the time lag between assembly and sub-division, what agent was responsible for assembly, and the time between which the final developer acquired the land and the time sub-division approval was applied for.

The results of both empirical studies suggest that the structure of the Toronto land market is consistent with the version of our theoretical models in which (*a*) the land market is competitive, and (*b*) there is a high degree of uncertainty. We will, therefore, proceed to use such a model in analysing the possible effects of public policy.

THE ROLE OF THE GOVERNMENT IN THE LAND MARKET

The economic case for the role of the government in the land market of course lies in the inherent externalities arising out of location decisions, and in the necessity of the provision of various public goods (e.g., roads). The basis for this case is the argument that even competitive markets may not allocate resources efficiently in the presence of externalities or in the provision of public goods. By instruments such as zoning regulations, government agencies can therefore likely improve the economic efficiency of the land and housing markets. However, it is clear that government agencies do not regard economic efficiency as their only objective. Thus situations can arise in which economic and non-economic objectives are in conflict and government preferences require the sacrifice of full economic efficiency in pursuit of the most preferred feasible objective. Such decisions, given government preferences, are not 'wrong' or irrational (in a positive sense) so that the only role of an economist in such a situation is to attempt to quantify the economic costs of the sacrifice of economic efficiency.

However, in our opinion, government agencies sometimes adopt policies which sacrifice economic efficiency, not in order to achieve some more preferred objective, but because of a misunderstanding of the functioning of the land and housing markets and of the effects of their policies on these markets. For example, any policy which does not lower the demand for housing or increase the supply will not reduce the price of housing. Policies such as home buyer's grants increase the demand for housing and so increase the price of housing. In the short run, when supply is very inelastic, such a policy is also not likely to result in a significant increase in the number of consumers who can afford to purchase houses. Thus the rationale for the home buyer's grant program seems likely to have been based, at least in part, on faulty perceptions of the functioning of the housing market. Recent arguments supporting a change in tax laws which would allow the deductibility of mortgage interest seem to share this defect.

Besides sometimes adopting policies which are not consistent with objectives, government agencies are also not always efficient in their administration of policies, which can also result in an impairment of the economic efficiency of the land and housing markets. In the next two sections we will discuss what we think are two examples of this.

UNCERTAINTY AS A BY-PRODUCT OF GOVERNMENT INTERVENTION

Chapter 4 emphasized the role of uncertainty in determining the equilibrium pattern of prices and rate of land development. Some uncertainty in the land market comes from consumer behaviour and the general business climate. Population growth, the level of income, construction costs, and consumers' outlook toward the future all influence land prices and, therefore, variations in these variables influence land prices. Our research, however, has also demonstrated to us that a major source of uncertainty in the land market is due to the various ways that government is involved in that market.

First, the value of undeveloped land depends critically on its zoning status. Rezoning land from agricultural use to residential use can multiply the value of that land many times. Zoning is, of course, an important and socially valuable control given the externalities in land use. Further, optimal zoning policy will require changes in zoning laws as conditions change with the passage of time. However, both developers and planners have complained to us that both municipal and provincial governments often make what appear to be indiscriminate zoning changes and changes in official plans. (Planners who have certain commitments to existing plans may, of course, resist beneficial changes at times.)

An example of this was the Ontario government's declaration several years ago that certain land around Toronto was to form a greenbelt and was definitely not to be used for residential sub-division. To the extent that agents in the land market believed the provincial government, they made decisions contingent on this belief. Over the next few years, this greenbelt area was significantly changed. In such a situation agents who made decisions based on the original policy will bear the costs of decisions which are *ex post* incorrect. If, as we believe, the land and housing markets are competitive, these costs will eventually be reflected in the price of land and houses and the rate of development.

A second way that government can create uncertainty relates to the handling of sub-division applications. Long variations in the time taken for a decision (either yes or no), confusion about the standards applied to judging applications, or even expectations of a change in government all introduce uncertainty into the market. Similarly, a lack of coherent and stable plans for trunk servicing facilities (e.g., sewers) creates uncertainty about the supply of serviceable land and, therefore, uncertainty about future land prices.

In summary, any action by the government which increases the amount of uncertainty faced by agents in the land market will necessarily increase the frequency of incorrect decisions by these agents, concomitantly increasing the costs of operation, which will be reflected in the price of houses and land and the rate of development. Therefore we would strongly recommend that government policies and their objectives be clearly stated, and that the costs arising from a change in policy be clearly recognized in any decision to change an existing policy. Notice that we are *not* arguing that policies should never be changed (we in fact advocate changes in some of the current policies), only that the costs of the changes be recognized and weighed in the decision.

THE SUB-DIVISION APPROVAL PROCESS

That the sub-division approval process is a proper and important government activity we do not dispute. But the social benefits obtained from land use control must be weighed against both the costs borne by taxpayers (costs of the necessary government bureaucracy) and the costs borne by the home buyer. Developers must incur very significant costs in dealing with this process, and these costs are in the end borne by consumers in the form of higher land and housing prices. Specifically, we would like to emphasize the following points.

The first point is that by controlling approvals, government can always slow the rate of development below the competitive rate. The theoretical analysis of chapter 3 suggests, of course, that this will raise current prices. But we should note also that if housing units have flexibility in design, raising present prices will tend to reduce lot and house size (which may or may not be desirable). Since houses are extremely durable goods, this will have a lasting effect on the stock of houses. The government must realize, therefore, that restricting sub-division approvals not only raises present prices but also leaves a mark on the housing stock for a long time to come.

The analysis of chapter 3 also emphasizes the effect that lot servicing costs have on development and prices. No small part of these costs are the manpower and time costs of the sub-division approval process. The longer that various government agencies sit on sub-division applications, the higher lot servicing costs will be. A $1,000,000 piece of land incurs either direct or opportunity costs of $100,000 per year at a 10 per cent discount rate. In a competitive market, these costs are eventually reflected in prices and the rate of development.

Sometimes the delays in judging applications simply result from bad administration. In other cases, they seem to result from conflicts within the government. It was suggested to us in interview, for example, that while the Ontario government was pushing applications in the early 1970s, some local municipalities were adopting no-growth attitudes and placing obstacles in the path of sub-division applications. Such a problem is more fundamental than bad administration since it originates in the conflicting objectives of different groups of people. This is a situation which is almost certain to arise out of any political process. Any policy which would speed the rationalization of different group's objectives would certainly enhance the economic efficiency of the development process.

Other ways that government can have an influence in this area relate to the way in which approvals are structured. For example, it was mentioned earlier in this study that once an approval is given, developers are generally under some pressure to proceed with development or risk cancellation of the approval. Given that the approval process is at present taking two years in many areas of Ontario, the market cannot respond quickly to unforeseen changes. If, on the other hand, developers were allowed to hold some stock of approved lots in reserve indefinitely, then a competitive market could react reasonably quickly in a situation where a speculative surge raised prices above long-run equilibrium levels. The net benefits of such a change in policy should be fully explored.

One final point deals with the relationship between the sub-division approval process and market structure. This is simply to emphasize the rather obvious point that the government influences the degree of competition in the market by its distribution of sub-division approvals across developers. It is important to recognize that demand and supply for land are intertemporal phenomena. The fact that only one developer chooses to develop approved lots in a given year is not sufficient evidence to imply the existence of market power. This issue was discussed in chapter 5 and it is suggested that the rules developed there are the proper ones for judging market structure when faced with the problem of distributing a limited number of approvals.

THE ONTARIO LAND SPECULATION TAX

The effects on the rate of development and on land prices of a capital gains tax on land holdings were developed in chapter 3. The model showed that the initial effects of the tax would be to increase development and thereby lower initial period prices. If a fixed supply of land is a binding constraint, however, an increase in development in initial periods must imply a decrease in development in later periods. This, in turn, must imply a higher equilibrium rate of price appreciation. It was emphasized that the government cannot expect both to increase the present rate of development and slow the rate of price appreciation using only this one tax instrument.

In chapter 4 we considered the effects of the Speculation Tax in a model including uncertainty and speculation. We argued that at least in the Toronto area, the short-run effect of the tax was beneficial in halting a speculative boom in the land market. However, the long-run effects of the tax are probably undesirable because the tax will lead to a change in the allocation of risk bearing, which would probably make the land assembly process less efficient, and possibly increase concentration.

The Ontario Land Speculation Tax,[1] which has been mentioned a number of times throughout this study, is far from being a pure capital gains tax. In its amended form it is a 20 per cent tax on gains without provisions to write off losses against tax liabilities. It also contains a number of loopholes that allow farmers (or companies carrying on farming) and developers to escape taxation. We will not discuss all of the provisions of the act here, but two important clauses need to be mentioned. First, if a developer subdivides and services land in a registered plan of sub-division subject to certain provisions of the Ontario Planning Act, there is no tax liability on the sale of that land. Sale of any other sub-divided and serviced land not qualifying under this provision is also exempt provided that the purchaser begins construction on all lots within 18 months of purchase. Second, if an individual or a company buys farm land and actively continues to farm the land, no tax liability is incurred. Further, if a farmer sells land to a non-farmer, the value of the house and eleven acres around the house is exempt, and the value of the remaining acreage is compounded at 10 per cent per annum from the original purchase date to arrive at an 'adjusted value.' It is this adjusted value which is then subtracted from the sale price to arrive at taxable capital gains.

Given these provisions, it is apparent that the tax is designed to discriminate against speculators and not against legitimate developers. Speculators can reduce their liability if they can successfully post as farmers[2] or if they normally acquire land so far before development that the above defined 'adjusted value' does not exceed sale price. But even if they can successfully pose as farmers, they will incur a tax liability upon sale to a developer if adjusted value exceeds sale price. It is important to note that this would have been the case in all of the speculative sales examined in chapter 6 except the sales by Nortonville Holdings and Armstrong in the Bramalea Assembly. If these empirical results are generally applicable, it is apparent that the role of speculators in land holding functions

---

1 The law which instituted this tax is officially called the Land Speculation Tax Act, 1974, and is found in the Statutes of Ontario, 1974, chapter 17. It was amended twice in 1974, and the amendments are found in chapters 107 and 121 of the Statutes of Ontario, 1974.

2 It is not clear to us if buying land and renting it out for farming (which is the normal situation) qualifies as 'carrying on farming.' If we are talking about a land holding corporation, 95 per cent of the company's assets must be in 'farming assets' (includes the value of the land) in addition to the requirement of actively carrying on farming if the company is to qualify for the exemption.

will be reduced. It was argued in chapter 4 that this shifting of risk will likely impair the efficiency of the development process by shifting relatively more risk bearing onto non-speculators. Thus if land assembly and risk bearing by middlemen is a productive economic activity (we think it is), the tax will increase the real costs of development and distort the price structure. Second, if the tax shifts a large amount of land holdings onto developers, land ownership concentration will increase.

We conclude, therefore, that the 20 per cent Ontario Land Speculation Tax will likely have three effects: (1) land holding will be transferred from specu-lators to developers, which will likely have significant effects on the land assembly process, (2) very little tax will ever be collected, (3) the effects on prices and the rate of development will be similar to a pure capital gains tax but less strong than a 20 per cent pure capital gains tax, and (4) concentration of holdings and large developers may increase. Note that the welfare of farmers will very likely decrease with the tax since they now must either bear the risk of holding their land longer to realize an expected increase in value, or sell for less than they could have received from speculators in the absence of the tax.

PUBLIC LAND BANKING

One commonly proposed policy which is intended to reduce land prices is government land banking. We will comment on this only briefly, since it is thoroughly discussed in Carr and Smith (1975). The main arguments advanced in favour of public land banking are: (a) public land banking is a means to control non-competitive pricing by providing an alternative supply of land; (b) public land banking will reduce land prices by supplanting the economic role and costs of speculation in the land assembly process; and (c) the government should be less risk averse and can forecast the future better than private agents in the land market, so it would be more efficient for the government to bear the risks of the assembly process and so reduce the uncertainty faced by the private sector.

Let us consider each of these arguments briefly. A public land bank could exert downward pressure on non-competitive land prices, if the land bank was large enough. However, the process of accumulating the land bank will raise land prices. A perfect example of this result is the Ontario government's recent assembly of land for the North Pickering Project in the Toronto area. Therefore in urban areas where concentration of ownership is a problem, the assembly of a public land bank is probably not the appropriate policy measure.

In a competitive land market speculators do make the land assembly process more efficient and they therefore earn a return for this function. It is sometimes argued that the costs of land assembly can be reduced if the government were to do the land assembling, since it has power of expropriation. There is some confusion in this argument. Part of the basis of this argument seems to be that speculative activity itself raises prices. This is not correct, at least in the long run. What is true is that the costs of land assembly, which are partially borne by speculators, are economic costs which are borne by the economy. Thus the argument for land banking must be made on the basis that the government can assemble land more efficiently than the private sector. Because of the political considerations which inevitably come into the expropriation process, this argument seems dubious. Certainly the recent example of the Ontario government's North Pickering Project land assembly casts considerable doubt on the proposition that the government can assemble land more efficiently than the private sector.

In the abstract, the last of the main arguments for public land banking has the most validity. It is sometimes argued that the government has a useful economic role in some competitive markets in which uncertainty is present. The basis of this argument is that government is able to pool risks more efficiently than the private sector. An argument of this kind is made in the context of an analysis of the criteria for public investment decisions by Arrow and Lind (1970). However, some of the Ontario government's recent forays into the land market (e.g., the North Pickering Project) have certainly increased, rather than reduced the level of uncertainty faced by agents in the land market. In summary, we do not find these arguments supporting public land banking to be persuasive.

CONCLUDING COMMENTS

This study was motivated in part by the tremendous increases in lot prices that occurred in Ontario in the early 1970s. Spurr (1974) estimated that pure rents on building lots reached as high as $66,000 per acre. Widespread public opinion and a number of government officials blamed these price increases on monopoly elements in the land market and on speculators. One of these officials was the president of the Central Mortgage and Housing Corporation of Canada,[3] an organization whose policies can have tremendous impact on the land market. We have shown here that the monopoly power theory did not hold up in Toronto during this period and that while there was an excess of speculative activity, we

---

3 Mr William Teron, President of the Central Mortgage and Housing Corporation, identified concentration of land ownership by big developers as a prime problem in an article
written by Mark Rickets for the Toronto *Financial Post*, 6 March 1976, p 12. In all fair-
ness, he was presumably talking about Canada in general and there may be evidence of
high concentration in some urban areas.

have argued that in the long run speculators cannot cause prices to deviate from competitive levels.

An alternative theory of the price surge during this period has been advanced by developers, realtors, and some planners and other government officials. This theory proposes that the price increases were caused by (*a*) unforeseen increases in demand, (*b*) an unforeseen shortage of trunk servicing capacity, especially sewers, and (*c*) an unforeseen unwillingness on the part of some municipalities to grant sub-division approvals. These problems then caused a price surge that was accented by an excess of speculative activity. Everything we have learned in the course of our study suggests to us that this is the correct theory.

The point we wish to emphasize here is that the implications that these different theories have for optimal public policy are radically different. If we accept the monopoly-speculation theory, presumably the best policy is to break up the monopoly and tax speculators heavily. If we accept the second theory, the optimal policy to reduce prices is simply to increase trunk servicing capacity and expedite sub-division approvals. We do have data for the York region which showed a large number of applications pending during the early 1970s and were told in interviews that the majority would be held up or killed by local municipalities. The amount of undeveloped land around Toronto within 45 minutes commuting time of the core is in excess of 80,000 acres. This figure is well in excess of the amount that will be required for development in the next thirty years in the absence of servicing or sub-division approval constraints. The problem has been that only a very small percentage of this land has been available for development, and we are led to the conclusion that Ricardian rents of $66,000 per acre for building lots were caused by government restrictions and not by a scarcity of undeveloped land per se.

We hope that the results of our study will persuade the proponents of the monopoly-speculation theory to reconsider their views concerning the causes of land price inflation in the 1970s. We also hope that we have contributed something to the understanding of the process of land development. Perhaps more importantly, we would like to think that we have helped convince some government officials of the tremendous importance in correctly understanding the causes of a problem before applying symptomatic treatment. Public policy is quite capable of making problems worse if it is based on an incorrect interpretation of underlying causality.

Land and housing price data

In the following Tables A.1 and A.2 we present data which illustrate the rise in land and house prices in Canada during the 1970s.

The data in Table A.1 break down production costs for new single family detached units in Toronto which are financed under NHA. These figures should not be interpreted as a definitive time series on construction and land costs because houses financed under NHA are not completely representative of the majority of new houses constructed. One problem is that NHA-financed houses are probably inexpensive relative to the majority of new houses constructed. Furthermore, the over-all rise in house prices caused some economizing in both the construction costs of the house and the size of the lot, so that the type of house and size of lot (and location of lot) typical in 1975 is probably different from that which was typical in 1972. In particular, the series on land costs significantly understates the trend in lot prices.[1]

The data in Table A.2 are the average dollar value per Multiple Listing Service (MLS) transaction for the first six months of the years 1972-6. These data give a fairly accurate picture of the trend in house prices in different regions of Canada

---

1 The report on Land Assembly and Servicing of Land (popularly known as the Comay Report) prepared for the Advisory Task Force on Housing Policy (Government of Ontario) indicates that lot prices increased by more than 100 per cent between spring 1972 and spring 1973. This report also indicated that the prices of homes in the $30,000 to $35,000 range in Toronto (1972) increased by approximately $15,000, with about two-thirds of this increase attributable to an increase in lot value.

TABLE A.1

Estimated production costs of new single-family detached units financed under NHA for Toronto (CMHC data)

Year	Total costs	Percentage increase	Land costs	Percentage increase
1965	19,677		5777	
1966	23,056	17.2	7097	22.8
1967	24,878	7.9	8306	17.0
1968	26,547	6.7	8834	6.4
1969	28,644	7.9	9667	9.4
1970	29,914	4.4	10,639	10.1
1971	32,567	8.9	12,294	15.6
1972	32,035	−1.6	11,507	−6.4
1973	36,218	13.1	13,261	15.2
1974	62,254	71.9	19,596	47.8
1975	57,098	−8.3	24,377	24.4

over the period. The only problem with the data arises from fluctuations in the percentage of total transactions that were conducted through MLS and in shifts in the composition of price classes of houses.

TABLE A.2

MLS statistics[1] (first six months, 1972-76)

	Average dollar value per MLS transaction for the first six months of the year					% change				
	1972	1973	1974	1975	1976	73/72	74/73	75/74	76/75	76/72
Canada	26,139	29,988	40,744	44,788	51,271	14.7	35.9	9.9	14.5	96.1
Br. Columbia	24,971	29,519	41,973	49,459	54,952	18.2	42.2	17.8	11.1	120.1
Alberta	24,476	27,745	36,403	44,115	63,105	13.4	31.2	21.1	43.0	157.8
Saskatchewan	16,193	18,670	23,172	30,637	44,634	15.3	24.1	32.2	45.7	175.6
Manitoba	19,379	20,161	25,830	32,143	38,436	4.0	28.1	24.4	19.6	98.3
Ontario	28,821	34,047	46,739	49,356	53,332	18.1	37.3	5.6	8.1	85.0
Quebec	25,699	26,195	32,505	33,462	37,943	1.9	24.1	2.9	13.4	47.6
Atlantic Prov.	23,331	24,071	29,397	34,113	37,434	3.2	22.1	16.0	9.7	60.4
Vancouver	29,921	38,562	57,303	63,169	68,944	28.9	48.6	10.2	9.1	130.4
Victoria	24,885	29,952	46,783	50,783	59,624	20.4	56.2	8.6	17.4	139.6
Calgary	24,850	28,575	38,793	45,741	72,392	15.0	35.8	17.9	58.3	191.3
Edmonton	24,887	27,423	35,877	43,739	58,884	10.2	30.8	21.9	34.6	136.6
Regina	16,707	19,800	24,526	32,103	41,276	18.5	23.9	30.9	28.6	147.1
Saskatoon	16,714	19,055	23,741	31,099	54,443	14.0	24.6	31.0	75.1	225.7
Winnipeg	19,471	20,244	26,054	32,297	38,802	4.0	28.7	24.0	20.1	99.3
Hamilton	27,035	31,788	42,511	44,342	50,050	17.6	33.7	4.3	12.9	85.1
Toronto	33,378	41,264	55,225	57,645	60,979	23.6	33.8	4.4	5.8	82.7
Montreal	24,983	25,768	32,968	34,137	38,788	3.1	27.9	3.5	13.6	55.3
Halifax	24,937	25,355	30,329	34,645	39,054	1.7	19.6	14.2	12.7	56.6
Saint John	21,208	22,656	28,650	34,267	38,000	6.8	26.5	19.6	10.9	79.2

1 These data were released by the Canadian Real Estate Association in 1976.

Ownership concentration and market power: the mathematical analysis

THE MODEL

Since consumers are identical, in equilibrium all will achieve the same utility level, independent of where they live. Therefore, if we let $V[r(x), w - T(x)]$ denote the indirect utility function of the representative consumer, the equilibrium rent profile, $r(x)$, must satisfy

$$V[r(x), w - T(x)] = \bar{v}, \tag{B.1}$$

where $\bar{v}$ is as yet undetermined. From (B.1), $r = r(x;\bar{v})$, and it is easily shown that $\partial r/\partial x < 0$, $\partial r/\partial \bar{v} < 0$. Notice that (B.1) is independent of the structure of the land market.

Let $h(r(x;\bar{v}), w - T(x)) = h(r(x;\bar{v}), x)$ be the demand for housing of a consumer living at distance x from the CBD. Then, by the usual properties of the indirect utility function,

$$h(r(x;\bar{v}), x) = -V_r / V_w. \tag{B.2}$$

It is easily seen that $dh/dx > 0$.

Let there be $n(x)dx$ consumers residing in the circular ring whose inner radius is $R + x$ and whose outer radius is $R + x + dx$. Their total demand for the housing composite in that ring is $h(x)n(x)dx$. Since this composite is measured by lot size, assuming for technical convenience that all land is available for housing, the total *potential* supply of the composite in this ring is $2\pi(x + R)dx$.

To allow for the possibility that for some market structures land may be held off the market for some rings, let $\theta(x)$ be the proportion of the land in the ring actually occupied in equilibrium. Then, in equilibrium we must have $h(x)n(x)dx = 2\pi\theta(x)(x + R)dx$, which we can write $n(x) = 2\pi\theta(x)(x + R)/h(x)$.

Let $\bar{x}$ be the solution of the equation

$$w - T(x) = 0, \tag{B.3}$$

i.e., $\bar{x}$ is the distance from the CBD at which transportation costs exhaust income. Then clearly whatever the market structure, the maximum radius of the city is $\bar{x} + R$. Now we can write the equilibrium condition for space as

$$N = \int_{o}^{\bar{x}} n(x)dx = 2\pi\int_{o}^{\bar{x}} [\theta(x)(x + R) / h(x)]dx. \tag{B.4}$$

This equilibrium condition is also independent of market structure.

PERFECT COMPETITION

If the equilibrium rent gradient is $r^*(x)$, then the rent per unit accruing to owners of land which is at distance x from the CBD is $r^*(x) - C(x)$ (for land actually occupied). Assuming that the land market is competitive, and that the only economic use of land is for housing, if $r^*(x) - C(x) > 0$ then all land in the ring with inner radius $R + x$ and outer radius $R + x + dx$ will be occupied in equilibrium. Thus, the remaining equilibrium condition for a competitive market is

$$\theta(x) = \begin{cases} 1, \text{ for } x \leqq x^c \\ 0, \text{ for } x > x^c \end{cases} \tag{B.5}$$

where x^c is defined as the solution of $r(x^c;\bar{v}^c) = C(x^c)$. Then $R + x^c$ is the equilibrium radius of the city.

This equilibrium is depicted in Figure 1, where $r^c(x)$ is the equilibrium rent gradient. Notice that the vertical distance between $r^c(x)$ and $C(x)$ at any x is the *Ricardian rent* earned by owners of land which is at distance x from the CBD.

MONOPOLY

Given the rent gradient, $r(x;\bar{v})$, the revenue derived from selling $\theta(x)$ of the land in a ring with inner radius $R + x$ and outer radius $R + x + dx$ is $2\pi\theta(x)(R + x)$ $[r(x;\bar{v}) - C(x)]$. Thus the remaining equilibrium condition becomes

$$\{\theta(x), x^{m}, \bar{v}\} 2\pi \int_{0}^{x^{m}} \theta(x)(R + x)[r(x;\bar{v}) - C(x)]dx, \qquad \text{(B.6)}$$

subject to $0 \leqq \theta(x) \leqq 1$, and (B.1) and (B.4).

We can set up (B.6) as an optimal control problem in the following way. From (B.1), $r = r(x;\bar{v})$ and $dr/dx = T'V_w/V_r$. By (B.2), we can write this:

$$dr / dx = - T'(x) / h(r(x;\bar{v}), x). \qquad \text{(B.7)}$$

Now we can write (B.6) as a control problem with an isoperimetric constraint (B.4):

$$\{\theta(x), x^{m}, \bar{v}\} 2\pi \int_{0}^{x^{m}} \theta(x)(R + x)[r(x;\bar{v}) - C(x)]dx, \qquad \text{(B.8)}$$

subject to $dr/dx = - T'(x)/h(r(x;\bar{v}), x), 0 \leqq \theta(x) \leqq 1$, and

$$2\pi \int_{0}^{x^{m}} [\theta(x)(x + R) / h(r(x;\bar{v}), x)]dx = N.$$

Identifying $r(x)$ as the state variable and $\theta(x)$ as the control variable, the Hamiltonian for the problem is

$$H = 2\pi\theta(x)(x + R)[r(x;\bar{v}) - C(x) + \Psi / h(r(x;\bar{v}), x)]$$
$$- \lambda[T'(x) / h(r(x;\bar{v}), x)], \qquad \text{(B.9)}$$

where Ψ is the multiplier for the isoperimetric constraint and λ is the usual costate variable.

For our purposes, the only necessary condition for (B.8) which is of interest is that for each x, $\theta(x)$ is chosen to maximize H. Since H is linear in θ, this condition becomes

$$\theta(x) = \begin{cases} 1, \text{if } 2\pi(x + R)[r - C + \Psi / h] > 0 \\ 0, \text{otherwise} \end{cases} \qquad \text{(B.10)}$$

which we can write

$$\theta(x) \;=\; \begin{cases} 1, \text{ if } (r(x;\bar{v}) - C(x))h(r(x;\bar{v}), x) > -\Psi \\ 0, \text{otherwise} \end{cases} \tag{B.11}$$

Since Ψ can be interpreted as the costate variable for state variable N, and $H_N = 0$, it is easily seen that Ψ is a *constant*.

Of course $(-\Psi)$ can be interpreted as the marginal value of having 'one' more person living in the city, and $[r(x) - C(x)]h(x)$ is the marginal revenue from selling '*one' person* land at distance x from the CBD. Thus the interpretation of (B.11) is clear. However, it is important to notice that unlike the competitive equilibrium it is the marginal cost and marginal benefit *per person, not* per unit of land which determines the monopoly equilibrium.

We must now determine the sign of Ψ. Let $\bar{v}^m$ be the utility level achieved in the monopoly equilibrium and let $\bar{v}^c$ be the utility level achieved in competitive equilibrium. Of course it must be the case that $\bar{v}^m \leqq \bar{v}^c$. Let $r^m(x) = r(x; \bar{v}^m)$ be the monopoly equilibrium rent gradient and $r^c(x) = r(x; \bar{v}^c)$ be the competitive equilibrium rent gradient. Then, since $\partial r/\partial \bar{v} < 0$, $r^m(x) \geqq r^c(x)$ for all x.

Suppose $\Psi \geqq 0$, and let $\Gamma^m = \{ x \mid [r^m(x) - C(x)]h(x) > -\Psi \}$. Recall that $[0, x^c] = \{ x \mid r^c(x) - C(x) \geqq 0 \}$. Then, since $r^m(x) \geqq r^c(x)$, if $\Psi \geqq 0$ we have $[0, x^c] \subset \Gamma$, which means that the area occupied in the competitive city is contained in the area occupied in the monopoly city. To prove that this is not possible, let $\gamma(x) = [r^m(x) - C(x)]h(x)$. Then $\gamma'(x) = [r^{m'} - C']h + [r^m - C]h'$. If we define x_0 as the minimum x which solves the equation $r^m(x) - C(x) = 0$, then since $r^{m'} < 0, C' > 0, h' > 0$, we have $\gamma'(x) < 0$ for $x \geqq x_0$. Therefore, if $\Psi \geqq 0$, $\Gamma^m = [0, \hat{x}]$ where $\hat{x} \geqq x^c$. If this is indeed the solution of (B.8), then $\hat{x}$ is the solution of

$$\max_{\{\hat{x}\}} 2\pi \int_0^{\hat{x}} (r + x)[r(x;\bar{v}) - C(x)]dx, \tag{B.12}$$

subject to:

(i) $V(r,x) = \bar{v}$

(ii) $2\pi \int_0^{\hat{x}} [(x + R)/h]dx = N.$

From (B.12), (i) and (ii), it is easily seen that $\bar{v} = \bar{v}(\hat{x})$ with $\bar{v}' > 0$. Therefore we can write (B.12) as

$$\max_{\{\hat{x}\}} 2\pi \int_0^{\hat{x}} (R+x)[r(x;\bar{v}(\hat{x})) - C(x)]dx, \tag{B.13}$$

for which the first order conditions are

$$(R+\hat{x})[r(\hat{x};v(\hat{x})) - C(\hat{x})] + \int_0^{\hat{x}} (R+x)\,\partial r/\partial\bar{v}\,d\bar{v}/d\hat{x}\,dx = 0 \tag{B.14}$$

Since $\partial r/\partial\bar{v} < 0$, $d\bar{v}/d\hat{x} > 0$, the second term in (B.14) is negative for any $\hat{x}$, and since $[r(x^c,\bar{v}(x^c)) - C(x^c)] = [r^c(x^c) - C(x^c)] = 0$, the first term in (B.14) is negative for all $\hat{x} > x^c$. Therefore the solution of (B.14) is such that $\hat{x} < x_c$, and so we have finally proved that it cannot be the case that $\Psi \geq 0$. A monopoly equilibrium of the form required in (B.12) is compared with the competitive equilibrium in Figure 2. Since $\hat{x} < x^c$ and $d\bar{v}/d\hat{x} < 0$, $\bar{v}^m < \bar{v}^c$. But then it must be the case that $r^m(x) > r^c(x)$ for all x, since $dr/d\bar{v} < 0$.

Now, using the fact that $\Psi < 0$, we can examine the equilibrium structure of the monopoly city by analysing (B.11). The first obvious property of the structure is that since $\theta(x)$ never takes on a value strictly between zero and one, if the monopolist withholds land in any small ring, he withholds *all* land in that ring. Let us now consider $\Gamma^m = \{x \mid \gamma(x) > -\Psi\}$, for some $\Psi < 0$. Clearly, $\Gamma^m \subset \{x \mid r^m(x) - C(x) > 0\}$. As shown earlier, $\gamma'(x) = [r^{m'} - C']h + [r^m - C]h'$, and since $r^{m'} < 0, C' > 0, h' > 0$, then γ' is of indeterminate sign for x such that $r^m(x) - C(x) > 0$. But this means that Γ^m may *not* be of the simple form $[0,x^m]$, but instead, there may be rings of *unoccupied* land strictly within the outer boundaries of occupancy. Using the popular terminology, we will term this situation 'leapfrog' development, which is a phenomenon which seems fairly common in North American urban areas. As we have seen, under our assumptions this cannot occur if the land market is competitive. The reason this may occur is that withholding an 'acre' of land inside the city raises the rent gradient more than the amount it is raised by withholding an acre at the edge of the city. This differential may be high enough to overcome the difference in the rent foregone on the more valuable land inside the city.

In Figure B.1, (B.11) is used to depict a monopoly equilibrium where leapfrog development takes place. The equilibrium occupied areas are $[0,x_1], [x_2,x^m]$. To understand why leapfrogging may occur, let us examine $\gamma(x)$ in more detail. Clearly a *necessary* condition for leapfrogging to occur is that $\gamma'(x) > 0$ for some x. Differentiating γ we have

$$\gamma'(x) = [r^{m'}(x) - C'(x)]h(x) + [r^m(x) - C(x)][(\partial h/\partial r)r^{m'}(x)$$
$$- T'\,\partial h/\partial w]. \tag{B.15}$$

Figure B.1

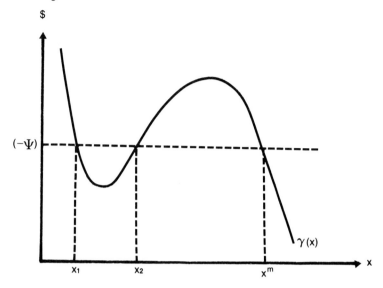

Since $r^{m\prime}(x) = -T'/h$,

$$(\partial h/\partial r)dr/dx - T' \partial h/\partial w = r^{m\prime}(x)[\partial h/\partial r + h\, \partial h/\partial w]. \qquad \text{(B.16)}$$

If we let $H(r,\bar{v})$ be the Hicks-compensated demand for housing, by (B.1), $h(r^m(x), w - T(x)) = H(r^m(x), \bar{v}^m)$. Furthermore, by the Slutzky equation $\partial h/\partial r + h\partial h/\partial w = H_r < 0$. Therefore, using (B.16), we can write (B.15):

$$\gamma'(x) = r^{m\prime}[H + (r^m - C)H_r] - C'H. \qquad \text{(B.17)}$$

Simplifying further, we have

$$\gamma'(x) = r^{m\prime} H[1 + (1 - C/r)\epsilon] - C'H, \qquad \text{(B.18)}$$

where ϵ is the price elasticity of demand of $H(r)$. Since $r^{m\prime} < 0$, $\epsilon < 0$, we see from (B.17) that γ' can be positive only in an elastic region of $H(r)$. Thus a *sufficient* condition for leapfrogging not to occur is that $H(r)$ be inelastic (for all relevant r). The intuitive explanation of this condition lies in the fact that the more inelastic is $H(r)$, the greater the relative difference between rents in the interior and the edge of the city. Thus the inelasticity of $H(r)$ makes the cost of foregone rent in the interior too large to make the benefit of withholding interior land profitable.

In Figure 2, we can compare the competitive rent gradient $r^c(x)$ and the monopoly rent gradient $r^m(x)$. Although this diagram was drawn on the assumption that leapfrogging does not occur, it is of course true that $r^m(x) > r^c(x)$ at each x, independent of whether or not leapfrogging occurs. In the diagram the distinction between Ricardian rent and monopoly rent can be clearly seen, since $r^c(x) - C(x)$ is the *Ricardian rent* and $r^m(x) - r^c(x)$ is the *monopoly rent* derived on land at distance x from the CBD.

'CONCENTRATED' OWNERSHIP

To analyse the typical case, for simplicity let us consider a model where there is one large landowner and all land he does not own is held in small parcels. Let $\alpha(x)$ be the proportion of land in the ring with inside radius $R + x$ and outside radius $R + x + dx$ which is owned by the large landowner. We will assume that $0 \leqslant \alpha(x) < 1$ for all x, so that there is competitively held land which is a *perfect substitute* for the large landowner's land at any distance x. If x^* is the greatest distance at which land is actually occupied in equilibrium, since the equilibrium rent gradient is downward sloping, all *competitively* held land at a distance of $\leqq x^*$ will be sold. Therefore the equilibrium configuration of the city is determined as the solution of

$$\max_{\{\theta(x),x^*,\bar{v}\}} 2\pi \int_0^{x^*} \theta(x)(R + x)[r(x,\bar{v}) - C(x)]dx, \tag{B.19}$$

subject to: $dr/dx = -T'(x)/h(r(x;\bar{v}),x)$; $2\pi \int_0^{x^*} \left\{ [1 - \alpha(x) + \theta(x)](R + x) \middle/ h(r(x;\bar{v}),x) \right\} dx = N$; $0 \leqq \theta(x) \leqq \alpha(x)$.

Forming the Hamiltonian, we have

$$H = \theta(x)(R + x)[r(x;\bar{v}) - C(x) + \Psi/h(r(x;\bar{v}),x)]$$

$$+ \Psi(1 - \alpha(x))(R + x)/h(r(x;\bar{v}),x) \tag{B.20}$$

$$- \lambda[T'(x)/h(r(x;\bar{v}),x)].$$

The first order conditions for the maximization with respect to θ becomes

$$\theta(x) = \begin{cases} \alpha(x), \text{ if } [r^*(x) - C(x)]h(x) > -\Psi, \\ 0, \text{ otherwise} \end{cases} \tag{B.21}$$

where, as before, it can be shown that $\Psi < 0$. As with the case of monopoly, we see that if the large landowner sells any of his land in some small ring, he sells it all. Although (B.21) is completely analogous to (B.11), the equilibrium configuration of the city depends critically on $\alpha(x)$. Since by assumption $\alpha(x) < 1$, it must be the case that $r^*(x^*) = C(x^*)$, since land is competitively held at all distances x. We will consider four cases.

Case 1: $\alpha(x) > 0$ for all x, such that $x_1 \leq x \leq \bar{x}, x_1 < x^c$

In this case the large landowner will necessarily withhold some of his land from the market, and so the equilibrium rent gradient will be raised above $r^c(x)$. The reason for this is that if he does not withhold any land, (B.23) will be violated for x near x^* since in equilibrium $r^*(x^*) = C(x^*)$. Therefore in this case leapfrog development will necessarily occur because by withholding some of his land the large landowner leaves unoccupied areas strictly within the boundaries of equilibrium occupancy. In particular, since $r^*(x^*) = C(x^*)$ he will withhold *all* his land 'near' x^*. This is because the 'marginal cost' of selling to one more consumer $(-\Psi)$, is always positive, but the marginal benefit of selling to a consumer near x^*, $\gamma(x^*)$, is zero. This result shows that even though land which is *perfectly substitutable* for the large landowner's land is competitively held, he still has market power, and by exercising it causes resources to be misallocated. Notice that the exercised market power of the large landowner raises rents on *all* occupied land, so that even competitively held land earns monopoly rents.

Let $\Gamma^c = \{x|[r^c(x) - C(x)]h(x) > -\Psi\}$, $\Gamma^* = \{x|[r^*(x) - C(x)] h(x) > -\Psi\}$, and let $A = \{x|\alpha(x) > 0\}$.

Case 2: $A \subset \Gamma^*$

If $A \subset \Gamma^*$ then the large landowner will sell all his land, so that the equilibrium is identical to the competitive city. Thus, although he has *potential* market power (i.e., he could affect the equilibrium rent gradient by withholding land), he does not exercise it. A *necessary* condition for $A \subset \Gamma^*$ is that the large landowner does not own land 'near' the boundary of the competitive city, a situation which seems very unlikely on the basis of observations of large developers' holdings. This is a necessary condition because if he does not withhold land, $r^*(x) = r^c(x)$, and so $r^*(x^c) = C(x^c)$, so that (B.21) would be violated for his land holdings 'near' x^c. This condition is not sufficient, however, since it could be the case that $[r^*(x) - C(x)]h(x) < -\Psi$ for $x \ll x^c$, in which case the large landowner would withhold land, again producing leapfrogging. Notice that $A \subset \Gamma^c$ is *not* a *sufficient* condition for all land to be sold, since although if he withholds any land, $r^*(x) > r^c(x)$, it is not necessarily true that $(r^* - C)h > (r^c - C)h$. Therefore if he owns *only* valuable interior land, it may still be optimal for him to withhold some of his land.

Case 3: $\alpha(x) = 0$ for $x \leq x^c$

In this case the large landowner will not be able to sell any land. In a dynamic framework however, if the city grows enough to encompass his holdings in the hinterlands, case 2 suggests that he will wait until the competitive boundaries are past the inner boundaries of his holdings before marketing any of his land.

We saw in cases 1 and 2 that if the large landowner *exercises* his market power, leapfrogging will *necessarily* result. This result however depended on the assumption that $\alpha(x) < 1$. If $\alpha(x) = 1$ for some x we have the following situation.

Case 4: $\alpha(x) = 1$ for $x_1 \leq x \leq \bar{x}, x_1 < x^c$

In this case the large landowner owns *all* the land near the boundary of the competitive city. If he does not withhold any land, then $r^*(x) = r^c(x)$, and so (B.21) is violated for his holdings near x^c. Therefore he necessarily withholds land, and $x_1 < x^* < \bar{x}$, so that he owns the occupied areas furthest from the CBD. The condition $r^*(x^*) = C(x^*)$ no longer holds, because no one else holds land near the boundary. In this case, as was true for monopoly, leapfrogging may not occur, since (B.21) may require only that he withhold land between x^* and $\bar{x}$.

As we saw in case 2, although the large landowner always has *potential* market power (except in the uninteresting case 3), he may not exercise it, so that the existence of a large landowner does not necessarily imply that a misallocation of resources will result. However, from cases 1 and 4 we can determine *sufficient* conditions for misallocation to exist. *If leapfrogging exists in equilibrium or if the large landowner owns land at the boundary of equilibrium occupancy, then there has been a misallocation of resources.*

QUASI-DYNAMICS

We will now interpret our static model and its results in the context of a growing urban area with the usual comparative statics methodology. We will assume that income in terms of the consumption good (w) and 'construction' and servicing costs in terms of the consumption good ($C(x)$) are constant, but that population increases over time. First we consider the effect of an increase in N on the equilibrium configuration of the competitive city.

From (B.1)

$$r = r(x;\bar{v}), \text{ with } \partial r/\partial \bar{v} < 0, \tag{B.22}$$

so that we can write the equilibrium conditions for the competitive city:

(i) $\displaystyle\int_0^L n[r(x;\bar{v}),x]dx = N$

$$\tag{B.23}$$

(ii) $r(L;\bar{v}) = C(L)$

Totally differentiating (B.23), we have

$$n[r(L;v),L)]dL + (\int_0^L n_r \, \partial r/\partial \bar{v} \, dx)d\bar{v} = dN \tag{B.24}$$

$$(r_L(L;\bar{v}) - C'(L))dL + r_{\bar{v}} \, d\bar{v} = 0.$$

Solving for $\partial L/\partial N$ and $\partial \bar{v}/\partial N$ from (B.24),

(i) $\partial L/\partial N = r_{\bar{v}} \, / \, [n(L)r_{\bar{v}} - (r_L(L) - C'(L))(\displaystyle\int_0^L n_r \, \partial r/\partial \bar{v} \, dx)]$

$$\tag{B.25}$$

(ii) $\partial \bar{v}/\partial N = -(r_L(L) - C'(L)) \, / \, [n(L)r_{\bar{v}} - (r_L(L)$

$$- C'(L))(\int_0^L n_r \, \partial r/\partial \bar{v} \, dx)].$$

Since $n(r,x) = 1/h(r,x)$, $\partial n/\partial r = -h_r/h^2$, which is > 0, assuming housing is a normal good.[1] Also, $r_{\bar{v}} < 0$, and $r_L(L) = r'(L) < 0$, so that

---

1 For the competitive equilibrium to be non-degenerate ($X^c \neq 0$), it must be the case that

$$\int_0^L n_r \, \partial r/\partial \bar{v} \, dx < 0.$$

$$\partial L/\partial N > 0, \; \partial \bar{v}/\partial N < 0. \tag{B.26}$$

Therefore,

$$\partial r/\partial N = (\partial r/\partial \bar{v})(\partial \bar{v}/\partial N) > 0. \tag{B.27}$$

Thus we see that the effect of an increase in N on the equilibrium competitive city is to increase the size of the city, lower all citizens' well-being, increase density at every x, and increase the equilibrium rent at every distance x. This can easily be seen in Figure I, using the fact that $\partial r/\partial N > 0$.

Now let us consider the effect of an increase in population on the monopoly city. As with the competitive city, it is clear that when N increases, $\bar{v}^m$ will fall and so $r^m(x)$ will rise at every x. Since the rent gradient shifts up, intuition suggests that the size of the monopoly city will increase, and in particular, previously 'leapfrogged' areas will fill in. To analyze this conjecture we must consider (B.11). Since $(-\Psi)$ is the marginal value of additional population, we would expect that the usual case would be that $\partial(-\Psi)/\partial N \leq 0.$[2] Again, letting $\gamma(x;\bar{v}) = [r(x;\bar{v}) - C(x)]h(r(x;\bar{v}), x),$

$$\partial \gamma/\partial \bar{v} = r_{\bar{v}} \, [h + (r - C)h_r], \tag{B.28}$$

which we can write

$$\partial \gamma/\partial \bar{v} = r_{\bar{v}} \, h[1 + (1 - C/r)E], \tag{B.29}$$

where E is the price elasticity of demand of $h(r)$. Therefore a sufficient condition for $\partial \gamma/\partial N > 0$ is that $h(r)$ is inelastic. Since $E < \epsilon$ if h is a superior good, then if $E \geq -1$, leapfrogging will not occur[3] and the city will grow as N grows. However, if leapfrogging occurs, then $\epsilon \ll -1$ for some x, and so $E \ll -1$ for some x. In this case, by (B.29) we may have $\partial \gamma/\partial N < 0$ for some x, and therefore some previously occupied areas may become vacant as N grows. By (B.11), for 'small' changes in N, these previously occupied areas will have been adjacent to vacant areas, so that if leapfrogging occurred, as N grows the 'leapfrogged' areas may *increase* in size!

---

2 If we let $\beta(N)$ be the maximized value of monopoly profits, then clearly $\beta(N) \leq wN$, suggesting $\partial(-\Psi)/\partial N \leq 0$ is the likely case, at least for 'large' N. If $\partial(-\Psi)/\partial N > 0$ the monopoly city might shrink with an increase in N.

3 See equation (B.18) and associated discussion.

The analysis of the growing city with concentrated ownership is identical to that for the monopoly city. However, it is of interest to note that in case 2 (all land sold by the large landowner), an increase in N may cause the large landowner to now withhold land, since, although r will rise, γ may fall sufficiently so that (B.21) no longer holds for some of the previously sold land.

APPENDIX C

Properties of the demand functions

The consumer's demand functions are given as the solution of the problem:

$$\text{Max } U_0(C_0,L_0) + U_1(C_1,L_0 + L_1), \tag{C.1}$$

$$\text{s.t. } (Y_0 + Y_1(1+i)^{-1} - C_0 - C_1(1+i)^{-1} - p_0 L_0 - p_1(1+i)^{-1} L_1) = 0,$$

$$C_0,L_0,C_1,L_1 \geq 0.$$

The first order necessary conditions for a maximum are given as follows:

$$\partial/\partial C_0 = U_{01} - \lambda \leq 0, \tag{C.2}$$

$$\partial/\partial L_0 = U_{02} + U_{12} - \lambda p_0 \leq 0,$$

$$\partial/\partial C_1 = U_{11} - \lambda(1+i)^{-1} \leq 0,$$

$$\partial/\partial L_1 = U_{12} - \lambda p_1(1+i)^{-1} \leq 0,$$

plus the constraint condition. Two results are of particular interest:

$$(U_{02} + U_{12})/U_{01} = p_0 \text{ if } C_0,L_0 > 0; \tag{C.3}$$

$$\text{if } p_0 - p_1(1+i)^{-1} \leq 0 \text{ then } L_1 = 0.$$

The first equation in (C.3) states that the marginal rate of substitution between L_0 and C_0 will be less than p_0. Since L_0 also gives utility at $T = 1$, L_0 is purchased past the point where the usual marginal rate of substitution condition holds. The second equation in (C.3) states that if the price of land is growing as fast as the rate of interest, consumers will wish to purchase all land in $T = 0$ since the cost of borrowing is less than the costs imposed by price appreciation.

The solution to the consumer's choice problem is shown in Figure C.1, where it is assumed for convenience that $Y_0 = Y_1$, $p_0 = p_1$, and that the consumer does not choose to borrow or lend. The budget line in $T = 0$ is given by Y_0B and the optimal consumption bundle, characterized by the marginal rate of substitution less than the price ratio, in $T = 0$ is given by A. The consumption bundle for $T = 1$ is found by shifting the budget line to Y_1B'. The optimal consumption bundle is now given by point A' with purchases of land in $T = 1$ equal to $(L_1' - L_0)$. The sum of U_0 and U_1 give the consumer's total welfare from this allocation. Borrowing an amount X at $T = 0$ can be conveniently represented in this diagram by a parallel shift out of Y_0B an amount X on the vertical axis and a parallel shift of Y_1B' equal to $X(1 + i)$ in the opposite direction.

Now we will discuss the comparative statics properties of the demand functions. A difficulty is that even the assumptions that land in each period is a normal good and that the composite consumption good is a net substitute for land in each period may not guarantee one property of demand that we have assumed. This is the property that a rise in p_0, *ceteris paribus*, reduces the total two-period demand for land $[\partial(L_0 + L_1)/\partial p_0 < 0]$. We will analyze this property for an individual consumer's demand functions. The problem then is that if L_0 and L_1 are gross substitutes, the (positive) pure-cross-substitution effect $(\partial L_1/\partial p_0)_{\bar{u}}$ may outweigh the (negative) pure-own-substitution effect $(\partial L_0/\partial p_0)_{\bar{u}}$ and the income effects $L_0(\partial L_i/\partial Y_0)$. It can be shown, however, that this possibility ceases to exist if the equilibrium rate of price appreciation is high enough.

A well-known demand theorem states that the sum of price-weighted pure-substitution effects must equal zero. In this context, that reduces to

$$p_0(\partial L_0/\partial p_0)_{\bar{u}} + p_1(1 + i)^{-1}(\partial L_1/\partial p_0)_{\bar{u}} + (\partial C_0/\partial p_0)_{\bar{u}}$$
$$+ (1 + i)^{-1}(\partial C_1/\partial p_0)_{\bar{u}} = 0. \tag{C.4}$$

Since $p_0 > p_1(1 + i)^{-1}$ when the equilibrium is characterized by positive land sales in each period, the assumption that the composite consumption good in any period and L_0 are net substitutes $\{(\partial C_i/\partial p_0)_{\bar{u}} > 0\}$ is not sufficient to

Figure C.1

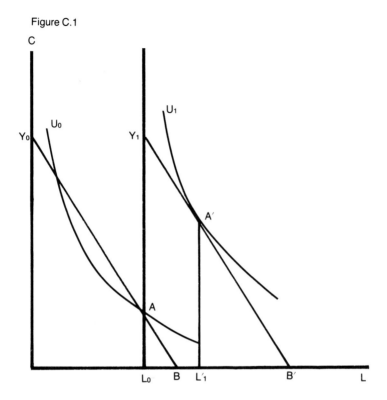

imply that the absolute value of $(\partial L_0/\partial p_0)_{\bar{u}}$ outweighs a positive $(\partial L_1/\partial p_0)_{\bar{u}}$. (The same argument does establish that $\partial(L_0 + L_1)/\partial p_1 < 0$.) The sum of the two effects, however, must become negative as the rate of price appreciation approaches i. Adding the influence of income effects then guarantees that, for a range of rates of price appreciation less than i, $\partial(L_0 + L_1)/\partial p_0 < 0$. It should also be noted that this property will hold for all rates of price appreciation that give interior solutions for many types of utility functions such as additive forms.

A second problem referred to in the section on market equilibrium deals with the possibility that all land will be withheld until $T = 1$. From the first order conditions in (C.2), a price configuration such that $L_0 = 0$ implies that $U_{02} + U_{12} - \lambda p_0 < 0$. Manipulation of these conditions gives us the result that $L_0 = 0$ and $L_1 > 0$ if and only if:

$$(p_1 - p_0)/p_0 < i - (U_{02}/U_{01})(1 + i)/p_0, \qquad (\text{C.5})$$

where U_{02}/U_{01} is the positive marginal rate of substitution between the composite commodity and land in $T = 0$. Similarly, the supply conditions given in (4) state that equilibrium will be characterized by $(L_0 = 0, L_1 > 0)$ if and only if:

$$(p_1 - p_0)/p_0 > r - [q(1 + r) + rs]/p_0. \qquad \text{(C.6)}$$

This equilibrium is less likely the higher the developers' discount rate relative to the consumers' rate and the higher the price of developed land relative to the return from agricultural land use. It should also be noted that with many commonly-used functional forms such as the Cobb-Douglas, the marginal rate of substitution U_{02}/U_{01}, becomes very large as L_0 approaches zero, implying that an equilibrium characterized by $L_0 = 0$ cannot exist.

Derivation of the effects of the taxes

THE PROPERTY TAX

Totally differentiating (10) and (13), we have

$$dp_0/d\tau - (1+r)^{-1}(1-\tau)dp_1/d\tau = (s - p_1)(1+r)^{-1}, \qquad (D.1)$$

$$(D_{00} - D_{10})dp_0/d\tau + [(D_{01} + D_{11}) + (D_{00} + D_{10})\tau(1+r)^{-1}]dp_1/d\tau$$

$$= -(D_{00} + D_{10})p_1(1+r)^{-1}.$$

Solving for $dp_0/d\tau$ and $dp_1/d\tau$ from (D.1) we have

$$dp_0/d\tau = [(s - p_1)(1+r)^{-1}[(D_{01} + D_{11}) + (D_{00} + D_{10})\tau(1+r)^{-1}] \qquad (D.2)$$

$$- (1+r)^{-2}(1-\tau)p_1(D_{00} + D_{10})] / \Delta,$$

$$dp_1/d\tau = -s(1+r)^{-1}(D_{00} + D_{10}) / \Delta,$$

where Δ is the determinant of the matrix of coefficients of (D.1).

Under our assumption that $D_{ij} + D_{ji} < 0$, it is easily seen that $dp_0/d\theta < 0$, $dp_1/d\theta < 0$.

THE CAPITAL GAINS TAX

Totally differentiating (15) and (6), we have

$$[(1 - \theta + r) / (1 - \theta)](dp_0/d\theta) - (dp_1/d\theta) = (p_0 - p_1) / (1 - \theta) \tag{D.3}$$

$$(D_{00} + D_{10})(dp_0/d\theta) + (D_{01} + D_{11})(dp_1/d\theta) = 0.$$

Solving for $dp_0/d\theta$ and $dp_1/d\theta$ from (D.3),

$$dp_0/d\theta = [(p_0 - p_1) / (1 - \theta)] (D_{01} + D_{11}) / \Delta,$$
$$\tag{D.4}$$
$$dp_1/d\theta = [(p_1 - p_0) / (1 - \theta)] (D_{00} + D_{10}) / \Delta,$$

where Δ is the determinant of the matrix of coefficients of (D.3). Again assuming that $D_{ii} + D_{ji} < 0$, we see that $dp_0/d\theta < 0$, $dp_1/d\theta > 0$.

Monopoly equilibrium: an example

This section will provide a simple analytic example that shows how the timing of land sales under conditions of monopoly will differ from the timing of land sales under conditions of perfect competition.

The demand functions for land in each period are assumed to be given by the following:

$$L_0 = \alpha_0 - b\,p_0 + \gamma b\,p_1, \tag{E.1}$$

$$L_1 = \alpha_1 - b\,p_1 + \gamma b\,p_0.$$

For the time being, it is assumed that $0 < \gamma < 1$.[1] α_1 might be larger relative to α_0 if, for example, consumer tastes shift in favour of housing over time.

For algebraic simplicity, it is assumed that agricultural opportunity costs and development costs equal zero. The monopolist's problem is to maximize the following function:

$$\text{Max } p_0(1+r)L_0 + p_1L_1 + \lambda(\bar{L} - L_0 - L_1) \tag{E.2}$$

$$= (\alpha_0 - b\,p_0 + \gamma b\,p_1)(1+r)p_0 + (\alpha_1 - b\,p_1 + \gamma b\,p_0)p_1$$

$$+ \lambda(\bar{L} - (\alpha_0 + \alpha_1) - (1-\gamma)b\,p_0 - (1-\gamma)b\,p_1) = 0,$$

1 This is equivalent to assuming that the pure cross substitution effect is larger than the absolute value of the pure cross income effect.

$$\partial/\partial p_0 = (\alpha_0 - 2b\,p_0 + \gamma b\,p_1)(1+r) + \gamma b\,p_1 - \lambda(1-\gamma)b = 0,$$

$$\partial/\partial p_1 = (\alpha_1 - 2b\,p_1 + \gamma b\,p_0) + \gamma b(1+r)p_0 - \lambda(1-\gamma)b = 0.$$

Manipulation of these first order conditions gives us the following relationships:

$$(1/\sigma)(\alpha_0(1+r) - \alpha_1) = \Delta p_0 - p_1, \qquad (\text{E.3})$$

where $\sigma = (2+r)\gamma b + 2b > 0$; $\Delta = [(2+r)\gamma b + (1+r)2b] / [(2+r)\gamma b + 2b] < (1+r)$.

A sufficient (but not necessary) condition for p_1 to be greater than p_0 is that the intercept term be growing faster than the discount rate r. Since $\Delta < (1+r)$, however, this is not sufficient for the equilibrium price ratio to exceed $(1+r)$, the ratio that will prevail in this example under competitive conditions.

The conclusion is that, with linear demand of this type, growth in demand below the market rate of interest will always lead the monopolist to supply less land in initial periods than would be supplied by a competitive market. On the other hand, for growth in demand sufficiently in excess of the discount rate, a monopolist will supply relatively more land in initial periods, leading to a rate of price increase in excess of the discount rate. Allowing the slope coefficients (b) and the cross effects coefficients (γ) to vary between periods will change the numerical values of σ and Δ in (E.3) but will not change the direction of the relationship, provided that $\gamma > -2/(2+r)$. γ can, of course, be negative if the pure cross substitution effect is less than the absolute value of the cross income effect.

A model of the consumer-speculator

A MODEL OF THE CONSUMER-SPECULATOR [1]

We assume that there is a single composite consumption good and two types of land, developed and undeveloped. The price of the composite assumption good is assumed to be unity at every time, and we assume there is a riskless asset which yields a rate of return r. As in the second section of chapter 4, we could include a non-land risky asset, but that would only make our exposition much more complicated.

Consider a consumer with a remaining life span of T periods, and a flow of wage income $\{I_t\}$, $t = 0, ..., T$. He consumes the composite consumption good and the flow of services from his holdings of developed land. He holds his wealth in the three possible assets, developed and undeveloped land, and the riskless asset. At any time t he will know the current prices of the two types of land, but is uncertain about future prices of land.

A simple model of the consumer's choice problem is given as the solution of the problem:

$$\max_{\{(C_t, L_t, \lambda_t, S_t)\}} E_0 \left\{ \sum_0^T (r + \rho)^{-t} U(C_t, L_t) \right\}, \tag{F.1}$$

subject to $C_t + P_t L_t + R_t \lambda_t + S_t = P_t L_{t-1} + R_t \lambda_{t-1} + (1 + r)S_{t-1} + I_t$,

$$t + 0, ..., T,$$

---

1 The analysis in this section is based on Samuelson (1969).

where C_t is consumption of the composite consumption good; L_t is the stock of developed land held, with P_t its price; λ_t is the stock of undeveloped land held, with R_t its price; and S_t is the amount invested in (or borrowed) in the riskless asset all at time t. E_0 is the expectations operator, where the expectations are over the future unknown prices (P_t, R_t), $t + 1, ..., T$. The subscript denotes the dependence of future expectations on P_0 and R_0. We assume that the utility function, $U(C_t, L_t)$, is concave.

The solution to (F.1) can be derived by dynamic programming in the following way. Let

$$J_1(W_1) = \max E_1 \left\{ \sum_1^T (1 + \rho)^{-(t-1)} U(C_t, L_t) \right\}, \tag{F.2}$$

subject to $C_t + P_t L_t + R_t \lambda_t + S_t = P_t L_{t-1} + R_t \lambda_{t-1} + (1 + r)S_{t-1} + I_t,$

$$t = 1, ..., T$$

$$W_1 = P_1 L_0 + R_1 \lambda_0 + (1 + r)S_0 + I_1.$$

Then by the Principle of Optimality, (F.1) can be rewritten:

$$\max_{\{C_0, L_0, \lambda_0, S_0\}} E_0 \left\{ U(C_0, L_0) + [1 / (1 + \rho)]J_1(W_1) \right\}, \tag{F.3}$$

subject to $C_0 + P_0 L_0 + R_0 \lambda_0 + S_0 = P_0 \bar{L} + R_0 \bar{\lambda} + I_0$

$$W_1 = P_1 L_0 + R_1 \lambda_0 + (1 + r)S_0 + I_1.$$

where $\bar{L}, \bar{\lambda}$ are the initial stocks of developed and undeveloped land held at the beginning of period o. Under the assumption that $U(C_t, L_t)$ is concave, it can easily be shown that $J_1(W_1)$ is a concave function of W_1.

We can now write the Lagrangean for (F.3) as

$$\mathcal{L} = U(C_0, L_0) + [1 / (1 + \rho)] E \left\{ J(P_1 L_0 + R_1 \lambda_0 + (1 + r)S_0 + I_1) \right\}$$
$$- \mu[C_0 + P_0(L_0 - \bar{L}) + R_0(\lambda_0 - \bar{\lambda}) + S_0 - I_0] \tag{F.4}$$

(where we have dropped the subscripts on E and J), and so the first order conditions for an interior solution of (F.3) are

(i) $U_1 - \mu = 0 = \mathcal{L}_{C_0},$

(ii) $U_2 + [1 / (1 + \rho)] E\{J' P_1\} - \mu P_0 = 0 = \mathcal{L}_{L_0}$,

(iii) $[1 / (1 + \rho)] E\{J' R_1\} - \mu R_0 = 0 = \mathcal{L}_{\lambda_0}$, (F.5)

(iv) $[1 / (1 + \rho)] E\{J'\} - \mu = 0 = \mathcal{L}_{S_0}$,

(v) $C_0 + P_0(L_0 - \bar{L}) + R_0(\lambda_0 - \bar{\lambda}) + S_0 - I_0 = 0 = \mathcal{L}_\mu$.

We can rewrite (i-iv) as

(i) $U_1 - U_2/P_0 = [1 / (1 + \rho)] E\{J' P_1/P_0\}$,

(ii) $U_1 = [1 / (1 + \rho)] E\{J' R_1/R_0\}$, (F.6)

(iii) $U_1 = [1 / (1 + \rho)] E\{J' (1 + r)\}$.

The interpretation of (F.6) is straightforward. These equations require that the marginal utility of a dollar of current consumption equal the expected marginal utility per dollar invested in the available assets. Notice that (i) differs from (ii) and (iii) because a dollar invested in L_0 also yields current consumption.

Although in a model with two or more risky assets almost anything is possible, we would expect that increased uncertainty would have predictable effects. For example, analysis of one risky asset model suggests that an increase in uncertainty (i.e., dispersion of the subjective probability distribution) would lead to lower demands for both types of land, if the expected rate of return on each type of land remained constant. This implies that for demand to remain the same, the expected rate of return on each type of land must increase with an increase in uncertainty. Therefore, since all land must be held by someone in equilibrium, an increase in uncertainty should lead to an increase in the expected rate of change of prices, and if expectations are correct, *on average*, the actual rate of change of prices will increase. By an identical argument, an increase in risk aversion (caused e.g., by a government policy which resulted in land holding being shifted towards more risk averse consumers) would tend, on average, to increase the average rate of change of prices.

The solution of (F.3) gives us the demand functions for land

$L_0 = L_0(P_0, R_0, I_0)$,

$\lambda_0 = \lambda_0(P_0, R_0, I_0)$. (F.7)

To determine the properties of these demand functions we must undertake the usual comparative statics analysis. Totally differentiating (F.5), we have the system of equations:

$$[\mathcal{L}_{ij}] \begin{bmatrix} dC_o \\ dL_o \\ d\lambda_o \\ -dS_o \\ d\mu \end{bmatrix} = \begin{bmatrix} 0 \\ \mu dP_o \\ \mu dR_o \\ 0 \\ (\bar{L} - L_o)dP_o + (\bar{\lambda} - \lambda_o)dR_o + dI_o \end{bmatrix} \qquad (\text{F.8})$$

where $[\mathcal{L}_{ij}]$ is the matrix of second partials of $\mathcal{L}$ with respect to $C_o, L_o, \lambda_o, S_o, \mu$. We have assumed here that the subjective probability distributions of (P_t, R_t) are not changed by a change in P_o or R_o. We will relax this assumption later. If we let Δ be the determinant of $[\mathcal{L}_{ij}]$ and Δ_{ij} the corresponding cofactor of $\mathcal{L}_{ij}$ we can solve for dL_o and $d\lambda_o$ from (F.8) by Cramer's Rule, which gives us

(i) $dL_o = \{[\mu \Delta_{22} + (\bar{L} - L_o)\Delta_{42}] / \Delta\} dP_o +$

$\qquad \{[\mu \Delta_{32} + (\bar{\lambda} - \lambda_o)\Delta_{42}] / \Delta\} dR_o + (\Delta_{42}/\Delta) dI_o,$ (F.9)

(ii) $d\lambda_o = \{[\mu \Delta_{33} + (\bar{\lambda} - \lambda_o)\Delta_{43}] / \Delta\} dR_o +$

$\qquad \{[\mu \Delta_{23} + (\bar{L} - L_o)\Delta_{43}] / \Delta\} dP_o + (\Delta_{43}/\Delta) dI_o.$

Let us examine (F.9 (i)) in more detail. We see that

$$\partial L_o / \partial I_o = \Delta_{42}/\Delta, \qquad (\text{F.10})$$

and

$$\partial L_o / \partial P_o \Big|_{[(\bar{L} - L_o)dP_o + dI_o] = 0,} = (\mu \Delta_{22}/\Delta) \qquad (\text{F.11})$$

which is the derivative of the *Slutsky-compensated* demand for L_o, so that (F.11) is the usual own substitution effect. Therefore we see that the comparative statics can be written in the usual Slutsky equation form

(i) $\partial L_o / \partial P_o = \partial L_o / \partial P_o \Big|_{\substack{\text{real income} \\ \text{constant}}} - (L_o - \bar{L}) \partial L_o / \partial I_o,$ (F.12)

(ii) $\partial \lambda_o / \partial R_o = \partial \lambda_o / \partial R_o \Big|_{\substack{\text{real income} \\ \text{constant}}} - (\lambda_o - \bar{\lambda}) \partial \lambda_o / \partial I_o.$

The second order conditions require that $\Delta_{ij}/\Delta < 0$, so that the own substitution effect will necessarily be negative. As always, the signs of $\partial L_o / \partial P_o$ and $\partial \lambda_o / \partial R_o$ will depend on the income effects. It seems reasonable to assume that $\partial L_o / \partial I_o$ and $\partial \lambda_o / \partial I_o$ are positive, although rational behaviour is certainly consistent with them being negative. Our derivation of (F.8) assumed that the (subjective) probability distributions of (P_t, R_t), $t = 1, ..., T$, did not depend on the (P_o, R_o). If we allow this dependence, (F.8) becomes

$$[\mathcal{L}_{ij}] \begin{bmatrix} dC_o \\ dL_o \\ d\lambda_o \\ dS_o \\ d\mu \end{bmatrix} = \begin{array}{l} 0 \\ [\mu - [1/(1+\rho)] \, \partial/\partial P_o \, E\{J'P_1\} \,]dP_o - \\ \quad - [1/(1+\rho)] \, \partial/\partial R_o \, E\{J'P_1\} \, dR_o \\ -[1/(1+\rho)] \, \partial/\partial P_o \, E\{J'R_1\} \, dP_o + \\ \quad + [\mu - [1/(1+\rho)] \, \partial/\partial R_o \, E\{J'R_1\} \,]dR_o \\ -[(1+r)/(1+\rho)] \, \partial/\partial P_o \, E\{J'\} \, dP_o - \\ -[(1+r)/(1+\rho)] \, \partial/\partial R_o \, E\{J'\} \, dR_o \\ (\bar{L} - L_o)dP_o + (\bar{\lambda} - \lambda_o)dR_o - dI_o \end{array} \qquad \text{(F.13)}$$

We can see from (F.13) that if expectations are changed by a change in (P_o, R_o), this affects (L_o, λ_o) through a pure substitution effect. However, the sign of even the own substitution effect is now ambiguous. Nevertheless, we would expect that the usual situation would have $\partial L_o / \partial P_o$ and $\partial \lambda_o / \partial R_o < 0$.

What is clear from (F.13) is that, at least in the short run, the effects on demand of 'shocks' in the land market will depend crucially on how expectations are formed. For example, the phenomenon of a 'speculative bubble' in which prices overshoot their long-run equilibrium level is perfectly consistent with 'rational' behaviour and the absence of market power. This sort of situation can arise when investors extrapolate past price changes to expected future price changes. Even casual observation of other asset markets indicates that this has not been an uncommon phenomenon in recent years. Two examples of probable speculative bubbles are the conglomerate boom in the stock market in the sixties, and the gold boom of the seventies.

Examples such as these should make clear that expectations can crucially affect short-run price levels and movements. However, in the long run we would expect there to be a rendezvous of prices with their long-run equilibrium levels, since faulty expectations will eventually be shown to be incorrect, and therefore will be revised.

QUALITATIVE PROPERTIES OF THE DEVELOPER MODEL

Assuming the equations in (42) in the text hold with equality, the qualitative properties of the developer model can be found by totally differentiating the equations in (42). These total differentials are

(i) $[1 - (1 + \delta)^{-1} \partial E \{P_1\} / \partial P_0] dP_0 = (1 + \delta)^{-1} \partial E \{P_1\} / \partial R_0 \, dR_0,$ (F.14)

(ii) $(1 + \delta)^{-1} \partial / \partial P_0 \, E \{(P_1 - s - R_1)f_1 + R_1\} dP_0 + (1 + \delta)^{-1}$

$\qquad E \{(P_1 - s - R_1)f_{11}\} d\lambda_0 + (1 + \delta)^{-1}$

$\qquad E \{(P_1 - s - R_1)f_{12}\} dX = [1 - (1 + \delta)^{-1} \partial / \partial R_0$

$\qquad E \{(P_1 - s - R_1)f_1 + R_1\}] dR_0$

(iii) $(1 + \delta)^{-1} \partial / \partial P_0 \, E \{(P_1 - s - R_1)f_2\} dP_0 + (1 + \delta)^{-1}$

$\qquad E \{(P_1 - s - R_1)f_{21}\} d\lambda_0 + (1 + \delta)^{-1}$

$\qquad E \{(P_1 - s - R_1)f_{22}\} dX = - (1 + \delta)^{-1} \partial / \partial R_0$

$\qquad E \{(P_1 - s - R_1)f_2\} dR_0.$

We can write this set of equations in matrix notation:

$$[Q_{ij}] \begin{bmatrix} dP_0 \\ dX_0 \\ dX \end{bmatrix} = \begin{bmatrix} c_1 \\ c_2 \\ c_3 \end{bmatrix} dR_0.$$ (F.15)

To analyse (F.15) we must make some assumptions about how expectations are formed. We will assume: $1 - (1 + \delta)^{-1} \partial E \{P_1\} / \partial P_0 > 0$, $1 - (1 + \delta)^{-1} \partial / \partial R_0$ $E \{(P_1 - s - R_1)f_1 + R_1\} > 0$, $E \{P_1\} / \partial P_0 > 0$, $\partial E \{P_1\} / \partial R_0 > 0$, $\partial E \{R_1\} / \partial P_0 > 0$, $\partial E \{R_1\} / \partial R_0 > 0$. Then, assuming p_1 and f, and R_1 and f are statistically independent, the sign pattern of (F.15) can be written

$$
\begin{bmatrix} + & 0 & 0 \\ + & & \\ + & [H_{ij}] & \end{bmatrix} \begin{bmatrix} dP_o \\ d\lambda_o \\ dX \end{bmatrix} = \begin{bmatrix} + \\ + \\ - \end{bmatrix} dR_o \qquad\qquad (\text{F}.16)
$$

where $[H_{ij}]$ is a negative definite 2 x 2 matrix. With this sign pattern it is easily seen that $dP_o/dR_o > 0$. What is happening here is that an increase in R_o, caused, for example, by an increase in consumer-speculator demand for undeveloped land, increases $E\{P_1\}$ which causes developers to slow down development at the original P_o, which increases P_o. The signs of $d\lambda_o/dR_o$ and dX/dR_o are indeterminate. This is because an increase in R_o increases $E\{P_1\}$ and $E\{R_1\}$. However, the most likely situation would seem to be $d\lambda_o/dR_o < 0$, $dX/dR_o < 0$.

Bibliography

Minor pieces of information were derived from more than one hundred references such as municipal plans, government-sponsored consulting reports, and private industry reports, such as those published by the Urban Development Institute. In order to conserve space these are not listed here.

Arrow, King. (1964) 'The role of securities in the optimal allocation of risk bearing.' *Review of Economic Studies*, 91-6
– and R. Lind (1970) 'Uncertainty and the evaluation of public investments' *American Economic Review*, 364-78
Bachelier, L. (1900) 'Theory of Speculation.' Reprinted in P. Cootner, ed., *The Random Character of Stock Market Prices* (MIT Press, 1964)
Bahl, R.H. (1968) 'A land speculation model: the role of the property tax as a constraint on urban sprawl.' *Journal of Regional Science* 8, 199-208
Bentick, B.L. (1972) 'Improving the allocation of land between speculators and users: taxation and paper land.' *The Economic Record*, 48
Brief on Design for Development (1972) Submitted by York Chapter of the Urban Development Institute to the Regional Municipality of York.
Carr, J. and L. Smith (1975) 'Public land banking: a theoretical approach.' (University of Toronto: unpublished research report)
Clawson, M. (1962) 'Urban sprawl and speculation in suburban land.' *Land Economics*, 38
Davidson, B.R. (1975) 'The Effects of Land Speculation on Supply of Housing in England and Wales' *Urban Studies* 12, 91-9

Dennis, M. and S. Fish (1972) *Low Income Housing: Programs in Search of a Policy.* (Toronto: Hakkert)

Development of Land Use and Transportation Alternatives (1974) (Toronto: Metropolitan Toronto Transportation Plan Review)

Friedman, M. (1965) 'In defense of destabilizing speculation' In *Essays in Economics and Econometrics* (Chapel Hill)

Harriss, C.L. (1972) 'Land value increment taxation: demise of the British betterment levy' *National Tax Journal* 25, 567-72

Land Assembly and Servicing of Land (1973) (Toronto: prepared for the government of Ontario, Advisory Task Force on Housing Policy (Comay Commission) by Kates, Peat, Marwick and Co.)

Land Inventory Survey – Zone 1 of the Toronto Centred Region (1973) (Toronto: Urban Development Institute)

Lewis, D. (1972) *The Corporate Welfare Bums* (Toronto: James Lewis and Samuel)

Morris, R.E. (1969) 'Fiscal controls of land monopoly.' *American Journal of Economics and Sociology* 28, 77-92

Mossin, J. (1966) 'Equilibrium in a capital asset market.' *Econometrica*, 768-83
— (1973) *Theory of Financial Markets* (Prentice-Hall)

Muller, A. (1976) *The Market for New Housing in Metropolitan Toronto* (Toronto: Ontario Economic Council)

Netzer, D. (1966) *Economics of the Property Tax* (Washington: Brookings Institute)

Neutze, G.M. (1973) *The Price of Land and Land Use Planning: Policy Instruments in the Urban Land Market* (Paris: OECD, Environment Directorate)

Nichols, D.A. (1970) 'Land and economic growth.' *American Economic Review* 60, 1065-83

Oates, W.E. (1969) 'The effects of property taxes and local public spending on property values.' *Journal of Political Economy* 77

Ohls, J. and D. Pines (1975) 'Discontinuous urban development and economic efficiency.' *Land Economics*

Performance and Impact of the Alternatives: Year 2000 (1975) (Toronto: Metropolitan Toronto Transportation Plan Review)

Performance and Impact of the Alternatives: Year 2000, Analysis of 1981 Travel Demand (1975) (Toronto: Metropolitan Toronto Transportation Plan Review)

Performance and Impact of the Alternatives: Year 2000, Analysis of Development Effects (1975) (Toronto: Metropolitan Toronto Transportation Plan Review)

Royal Commission on Metropolitan Toronto (1974) 'The planning process in Metropolitan Toronto'

Population and Employment Forecasts for 1981 (1975) (Toronto: Metropolitan Toronto Transportation Plan Review, Toronto)

Samuelson, P. (1957) 'Intertemporal price equilibrium: a prologue to the theory of speculation.' *Weltwirtschaftliches Archiv*, 181-219

— (1969) 'Lifetime portfolio selection by stochastic cynamic programming.' *Review of Economics and Statistics*, 239-46

Scheffman, D.T. (1976) 'A continuous-time model of a stock market value maximizing firm.' Unpublished

Scherer, F. (1970) *Industrial Market Structure and Economic Performance* (Chicago: Rand McNally)

Shoup, D.C. (1969) 'Advance land acquisition by local governments: a cost-benefit analysis.' *Yale Economic Essays* 9, 147-207

Smith, L.B. (1974) 'The Ontario Land Speculation Tax: an anatomy of an un-earned increment land tax.' University of Toronto Working Paper

— (1975) 'The Ontario Land Speculation Tax: an economic assessment.' University of Toronto: unpublished research report

Smith, R.S. (1975) 'Land prices and tax policy: review and analysis.' University of Alberta Working Paper.

Solow, R. (1973) 'On equilibrium models of urban location.' In M. Parkin, ed., *Essays in Modern Economics* (Longmans)

Spurr, P. (1974) *The Land Problem's Problem* (Ottawa: Central Mortgage and Housing Corporation)

Spurr, P. (1976) *Land and Urban Development* (Toronto: James Lorimer and Co.)

Stigler, G. (1968) *The Organization of Industry* (Homewood, Ill.: Richard D. Irwin)

Turvey, R. (1957) *The Economics of Real Poverty* (London: George Allen and Unwin)

Williams, J.B. (1935) 'Speculation and the carryover.' *Quarterly Journal of Economics*, 436-55